INVESTING

for the

SMARTER

SEX

TIFFANY KENT, CFP ®

Publishing Services provided by Paper Raven Books
Printed in the United States of America
First Printing, 2020

Paperback ISBN= 978-1-7357961-0-9
Hardback ISBN= 978-1-7357961-1-6

Table Of Contents

Dedication

To Alexandra, Caroline, and Henry:
Always invest in your dream life.

Introduction

Five years ago, I reached a crossroads: Should I continue my career as a portfolio manager or retire? Up to that point, I had built a pretty impressive resume and track record in the finance world. I graduated from a good college, got a good job, went to business school, and made money, all while raising three children with my husband. Even after achieving all this, at the age of 42 life and money for some reason felt more confusing and more chaotic than ever. I was wealthy but deeply unhappy. My career had followed a linear path, and now I felt off track and uncertain where to go next. Being unclear about money made me anxious, and I felt like I was falling behind. Four long years later, I had figured out a new path, which gave me the certainty that I had been longing for. But I wish I'd had someone to help guide me on what to do and how to navigate finances when they felt unpredictable. So, I decided to take everything I learned and put it in this book so that other women who are in my shoes don't have to figure everything out on their own. These strategies and lessons learned helped me generate personal as well as financial returns. I want to share them with you so that you have the power to change your life and wealth forever.

As a wealthy woman in today's complex world—whether you inherited money, earned it yourself, or got it in the divorce—at some point in your life you will likely be solely responsible for making all of your financial decisions. It's not just that women tend to have multifaceted financial lives; we also live longer, our careers tend to be more volatile, and we are more likely to care for children and aging parents. Statistics point to the necessity for women to develop financial prowess: At least half of marriages end in divorce, 80% of men die married while 80% of women die single, and women outlive their late husbands by 14 years. There is a 95% chance you will be the primary financial decision maker for you and your family.[1] Women in today's world have so much to juggle. We have careers,

---

1 Prudential Research Study, 2010–2011 "Financial Experience & Behaviors Among Women," Prudential Financial.

families, people to take care of, and our own sanity to maintain. Engaging with our money is just one more thing that gets added to the never-ending to-do list. Even when women do try to manage and grow our money, we tend to make costly mistakes! The reason? Most financial advisors do not ask you what is important to you. Instead, they usually focus on selling products and services to you regardless of your actual need.

Focusing on what you value, what's important to you, and how to engage with your wealth will lead you to invest in your life with meaning and purpose.

I spent decades working as a hedge fund portfolio manager on Wall Street, picking stocks and managing a large portfolio. The days of earning huge bonuses, having great investment calls, wearing expensive clothes, and looking out of my fabulous high-rise office window in New York City made me feel like the most powerful woman in the world! (And it didn't hurt to have a husband who bragged about my success.) I loved generating financial returns, but something was missing. I wasn't in control of my own success nor did I know how to define success, so I wasn't able to generate any personal returns even though I had money. Here's the secret: Success means feeling passionate about what you do, and you don't have to be a woman on Wall Street making money to feel powerful and to be in control. I'm here to tell you how you can have an edge in life and start living the dream. Knowing that your success is completely dependent on you is beyond scary at times, but let's just take it one step a time. First, figure out what you're excited to tackle when you wake up each day. What gets you out of bed each morning feeling motivated and energized? Then, you can start getting your financial house in order with financial planning, learning basics about investing, hiring an advisor, and following my easy-to-use guide to invest. Before you know it, you will be on your way to being in command like Wonder Woman, ready to take on whatever comes your way!

I am passionate about helping women eliminate money worries and take control of their wealth. I'm going to show you why you need to create your own vision of your future and how to design a financial plan, just as you would design your dream house. The truth is that you already have amazing insights into investing, you just don't realize it yet! Think of me as a fairy financial godmother. I'm going to show you how to invest with confidence so you don't have to worry about money again. You might come up with some common excuses, like "I don't need a plan," "I don't have time," and "I won't run out of money."

Excuses are not the stairway to success.

They take you on a twisted, windy road and eventually lead you to neglecting your money and prevent you from connecting your money with what you value. What I have learned is, if you open your heart to what you want and connect your wealth to the life you want to build, you can have both love and money in good times and in bad. Sounds impossible? It isn't.

Planning for your financial future is a lot like planning to become a mother. When you find out you are having a baby, you read every book and blog post you can find, research all the baby products and gear, and ask other moms for guidance. Oh, and you do all of this at breakneck speed, since the baby will be here in just a few months! But 99% of the time, we don't do anything to prepare ourselves for our financial future. Maybe because there isn't such a fast deadline; nine months until a baby arrives seems way more urgent than retiring in 35 years. It's easy to get caught up in the short-term, day-to-day worries of our lives instead of taking time to plan how we'd like to be living 10 years from now. But your financial future has two vital things in common with a baby: It's coming whether you're ready or not, and it will be with you the rest of your life. Sadly, most women I speak to don't do much of anything to prepare for their financial lives. And it's hurting them.

When I tell other women what I do, they all have stories of the woman they know who still needs her ex-husband to support her or who relies on her grown children even though they are financially strapped themselves. And there are too many stories about women becoming victims of financial fraud. Most of those women had one thing in common: They all believed they didn't need to worry about their money. It may be too late for these women, but it's not too late for you! You have to stop believing the lies we all tell ourselves. Thinking "it won't happen to me" or "everything will be okay" is the worst kind of lie. It's what we tell ourselves when we don't want to face the truth. The world is complex and full of variables you cannot control. Lives can change in an instant if your marriage ends in divorce, your husband develops a health issue, or your income source has the rug pulled out from under it. All of this requires you to think differently about your money and be prepared rather than wait until something happens.

You—and only you—are ultimately responsible for your financial well-being. Not your husband, not the economy, not the market, and please don't make your kids financially responsible for you when you get older, darling. If you don't take this responsibility seriously, you may end up working at an hourly job in your 60s. Would you say that's what you want to do in your golden years? Or would you rather spend a few hours today putting together a financial plan so you can live in your dream house without a worry in the world later in life?

Finance and investing are intimidating and complex, or at least it seems that way from the outside. What happens all too often is that we ignore our money and put our heads in the sand until something happens. Then we realize we need to figure it all out and are having to make decisions under immense stress. I was on this path myself five years ago, and what I was missing at that time was knowing what I wanted. I didn't have a plan or a dream. I didn't know my "why" when it came to money. Apple knows why they are in business. We know why we have babies and why we buy a house. So, do you know why you do what you do? Do you know what is important to you? Do you know what is in your heart and what you desire? Do you know your financial future? Women often don't get what we want because we don't ask for it and we women underestimate ourselves.

If you can't communicate the life you want clearly, then you either haven't thought enough about it or you are relying on others to plan your life for you. Nobody can figure out your why for you; only you can do that.

So, the first part of the solution is figuring out your why. The other part of the solution is learning from the most common mistakes people make with their money: They either (a) don't have a financial plan or (b) have an investment portfolio that isn't aligned with both the husband's and wife's financial future. Generally, the one-sided plans result from men mostly dictating their objectives while women are not included in these discussions at all. Women make 80% of the household spending decisions, so it's essential that we are included in planning our financial future.

Investment requires a certain amount of risk, so be prepared to step out of your comfort zone in order to ultimately live a life with less money stress. When you apply an investor's mindset in your day-to-day life, you have clarity on your direction in life and are leading with your heart. You see quite clearly what is most important for you to focus on, and this unclouded perspective puts your life in order. I believe that you will learn to love investing and the peace of mind that comes with securing your financial future for you and your loved ones. Through my own investment journey and all my wins and losses, I've learned what every woman should know about how to make your dream financial future a reality through smart investing. So, let's go do this!

Please note: If you have credit card debt, student loans, or any other kind of debt (other than a mortgage), I would strongly advise paying those debts off before beginning your investment journey.

Part One

🎀

FEMALE
FINANCES

Chapter 1

THE FOUR FANTASIES

—✦—

A mom is getting ready for a date, putting on blush and taking out her curlers while enjoying a glass of wine. Her daughter walks into the small bathroom and asks for help with her math homework. Mom, who is running late for her date, brushes the girl aside and tells her, "Honey, if you look like this when you grow up, you won't have to worry about math." The girl pushes back and says, "But I really like math. And the two cute boys at school, Joey and Tom, their dads work on Wall Street and they are super smart, and I want to work with boys like that on Wall Street." The mom looks at the little girl and says, "Wall Street? You can live this great lifestyle and not have to work a day in your life! Just marry well."

Does that story sound familiar to you? I know it sounds familiar to me because it's *my* story. I was that little girl, and that's the exact advice my mom gave me. My mother was already divorced from my father when she told me that. She was receiving alimony and was already on the hunt for the next rich man who would fund the rest of her life. Years later, my mom moved us to an apartment in Beverly Hills instead of buying a house and for the next 20 years spent her money like it was going out of style on expensive jewelry, big screen TVs, music recording equipment, a brand new RV, and a bunch of other stuff she didn't need. Meanwhile, I stepped up to be her personal chief financial officer in my early teens to keep the lights on. I would handle preparing and mailing the checks for our monthly bills and balancing the checking account to ensure that our power didn't get turned off (again).

Not only did I handle all the finances as a young teenager, I also handled literally other aspects of maintaining a home and my life. I did the dishes and laundry, made my own doctor's appointments, rode my bike to the grocery store, and managed my own separate bank account funded by my father who gave me a nice monthly allowance. Once I left for college and my mother's alimony ended, she was forced to move to a shitty apartment in a small town in California. She never remarried. My mother couldn't see beyond her current lifestyle. She thought that because she was attractive she could just marry again, and because she'd have a new husband soon that he'd take care of her financially. Instead, she remained single, ran out of money, and bought a bunch of stuff that is worthless.

The truth of the matter is that my mother's story is not unique. I meet many women who tell me their mother was just like mine. Most of my generation has to financially support their parents. We are from a different generation than our mothers', when it was much less common for women to work and divorce was less prevalent. Women primarily stayed home raising children because husbands made enough money to support the whole family. Times have changed. Now, we have to be prepared to take care of ourselves. So many women wait until something bad happens to force them to learn about their money. Some women stick their head in the sand and never learn about investing, either in themselves or in the stock market. Like my mother, some women might simply wait for things to get better and for more money to show up. One woman I know received a $10,000,000 settlement from her divorce but was spending $720,000 a year. Guess how long that $10 million will last if she continues to spend at this rate and not invest? (Spoiler: About 13 years. So much for retirement.)

Women like my mother illustrate what I call the Four Fantasies of Female Finance. These fantasies are:

1. I don't need a financial plan for my future. Everything will be fine!
2. I'll never run out of money. We have plenty!
3. I can always get more money if I need it!
4. My husband manages our money. I don't need to think about it!

The problem with these fantasies is that they're just that: *fantasies*. And the realities behind them can be pretty scary. Let's look at each one more closely.

1. I don't need a financial plan for my future. Everything will be fine!

There are so many things in life we can't control: death, divorce, disabilities. Let me tell you some unexpected realities that women have been forced to face:

- The husband marries the nanny.
- He develops a health issue and wipes away $1 million from her 401k.
- He asks for the engagement ring back three weeks before the wedding, costing her family over $100,000 for a wedding that didn't take place.
- He leaves a highly paid job to go teach his kids to become ski racers.
- The wife realizes she married the wrong person and wants a divorce.

Then there is the economy and the stock market. My husband and I have lived in the heart of the cities that experienced the burst of the bubbles: San Francisco during the dot-com bubble, New York during the financial crisis, Houston during the oil bubble, and now we are here in Atlanta living through a global health crisis. We have learned the hard way that we really can't predict what will happen nor when it will happen. And while it sucks to be so negative about our economy and politics, the truth is that we don't have the protection of pension and economic stability our parents had; instead we are faced with bubbles, rising healthcare costs, and growing income inequality.

While we do not know what will happen when, we do know that we can assess risks and protect ourselves from certain risks. For the risks you can't insure, you will need to develop some strategies to protect yourself and navigate these topsy-turvy times better than anyone else. And that means making a plan for your financial future by taking risk and investing.

2. I'll never run out of money. We have plenty!

I've noticed a trend around this fantasy: It's largely held by women who don't work outside the home. I actually get approached fairly often by successful men who ask me, "Can you talk to my wife about her overspending?" Nine times out of ten, the wife in question has a lot in common with my mother. The truth is that it's very easy to run out of money! Even if you aren't sitting around watching TV all day or spending $60,000 a month, running out of money is a very real possibility for many, many women. When the oil bubble burst while we were living in Houston, I was worried about my financial future and the possibility I might run out of money even though my husband had a successful career as a lawyer. And it wasn't just me who was worried. I started to connect and learn from women who had their own horror stories. Unfortunately, shit happens. Your husband might have medical problems and you don't have enough health insurance, forcing you to dip into your 401k to pay medical bills. Or your husband might die unexpectedly, and you learn he didn't have enough life insurance or didn't have insurance at all. Even though 60% of people do have life insurance, 75% of those people do not have enough life insurance to actually live on. More than half of people don't have a will. It's easy to outlive our money when we don't have enough clarity on our personal financial numbers to know what our future expenses will be and if we will have enough.

3. I can always get more money if I need it!

Well, this one might be true, but it also might not be that simple. I remember a close friend who worked with me in investment banking telling me in my early days on Wall Street, "Don't worry about money. You will make so much more of it in the future." Even though I didn't believe him, he was right! But a few years later, making more money was part of the problem. I became a portfolio manager at a hedge fund in New York City, which was a dream I thought I could never achieve. It gave me power and prestige in a world where only 3%

of portfolio managers are women. But after some ups and downs with the great financial crisis and a big move away from New York City, the center of the financial universe, I was out of my wheelhouse. After a successful career on Wall Street, what was I supposed to do next? Retire in my 40s and just raise the kids while investing our family money? Or work for someone else again? It was really hard at the time to figure out what to do. My good friend from business school, who worked in private wealth in Houston, decided to retire. She wanted time to work out and to be with her kids. But this plan didn't feel like the right fit for me. Why did I work so hard to just retire in my mid-40s? I would have regretted this decision if I had followed her lead.

I started researching and looking for guidance on how smart women navigate life and fulfillment. I came across a Harvard study on women who graduated from the MBA program, and their findings suggested that most women who graduate from Harvard Business School usually work part time when their husbands' careers take off.[2] But that wouldn't work for me, since Wall Street is not

---

2 Robin J. Ely, Pamela Stone, and Colleen Ammerman, 2014, "Rethink What You 'Know' About High-Achieving Women," *Harvard Business Review* (Dec).

a part-time job. You have to follow the market and stocks every day, so there are no days off. Plus, I didn't work this hard to reach this level of success just to work part time. Even if I did find something to do part time, I would fail because I would resent everyone around me working full time and I wouldn't feel like I was part of the team. Cutting back to part-time was out. So, while I could "just make more money," suddenly that wasn't so simple. It mattered more what I did to make the money and what made me happy, and at that point I had no idea how to make those two sides line up.

4. My husband manages our money. I don't need to think about it!

This is the most dangerous of the four fantasies, mostly because it's the easiest to buy into. Even the most successful women in the world tend to let their husbands manage their money. Even Sheryl Sandberg, Chief Operating Officer of Facebook, let her husband handle all of their money. Why is this fantasy so pervasive? I've asked friends both inside and outside of finance why more women aren't engaged with their own finances, and here are the typical answers I hear:

- I don't have time to worry about managing money. I'm already working full-time, raising kids, and managing a household.
- My husband makes the money, so he should be the one to manage it.
- We divide responsibilities: He deals with the money, I deal with the kids.
- It's how my parents did things, so it's what I know and what I'm used to.
- I never learned to manage money or invest, and he did, so I leave it to him.
- It's too complicated and I've got enough on my plate.

I also believe that, for many women, money can be a sore subject because we often give up careers and sacrifice making our own money to raise families. Going from bringing home your own bacon to not having any income can make you feel uncertain about money, your career, or what role you have to play. If you choose to stay home to raise the kids, not knowing if you will have enough money creates huge anxiety and keeps people up at night. It might be easier just not to think about it.

We all know we are not taught about personal finance or investing in school. We usually learn it from our parents or don't really learn it at all. People think it should just come naturally. Spend less than you make and invest what you save. Parents directly teach us this by the way they shop, make buying decisions, or talk about investing, yet sometimes later in life these lessons taught to us weren't enough and might get us into financial trouble. Or worse, parents never learned to talk about money, just like some parents avoid talking about sex, and so they are repeating the vicious cycle of how to make not-so-great decisions by not teaching you. Most parents don't take the time to talk with their kids about financial decisions and investing, and I think it's fair to assume that most women do not talk about investing with their kids. My mother certainly didn't.

But here's the unpleasant truth: There is an 80% chance your husband will die before you and a 50%

chance you will divorce. Maybe for some that is not a bad thing. But for a woman like Sheryl Sandberg, who lost her husband unexpectedly, she is now the main financial decision maker for her family. There's a 95% chance you will be the main financial decision maker in your life at some point.[3] And like my mother learned to her disappointment, simply waiting for another husband to come along won't solve that problem. As we get older, our financial lives get more complicated, and we feel overwhelmed with organizing our family's social calendar, activities, career, business, and house.

We don't take the time to understand the real risks in life we face nor do we take the time to understand the opportunities life has to offer, both of which are tied up in understanding and managing our money.

As strong, educated women, we busted our butts in school, we took chances in our careers by being true to ourselves, we decided who we wanted to marry, and maybe we had babies. Now what? If you have never thought about any of this, or if you've bought into any of these four fantasies, please don't be discouraged. It's not too late to become the financial maven you were meant to be! The first step is recognizing where you've bought into the

3 Prudential Research Study, 2010–2011 "Financial Experience & Behaviors Among Women," Prudential Financial.

idea that you aren't her, or can't be her, in the first place. Before you move on to the next chapter, take a moment to consider which of these four fantasies has been the most appealing for you.

1. I don't need a financial plan for my future. Everything will be fine!
2. I'll never run out of money. We have plenty!
3. I can always get more money if I need it!
4. My husband manages our money. I don't need to think about it!

What in your experience has drawn you to that fantasy? And what do you now recognize as the true reality that it's time to embrace?

Chapter 2

HE'S JUST NOT THAT INTO YOU

Financial advisors are a key component to successful investing and planning, yet the fact of the matter is that women have long been ignored and bulldozed when it comes to professionally managing finances. Too many think money is a man's game and women are not suited to play. When I was first hired at Credit Suisse First Boston's investment banking Los Angeles division, I was the only woman employee who wasn't an assistant, and even today there are relatively few women who work in finance and investment management. On top of that, most advisors have little to no experience managing money for female clients because wealthy women rarely seek professional financial advice (for reasons we explored in Chapter 1). More fundamentally, the financial management world is a male echo chamber, and the reverberating message throughout that echo chamber is time is money and it takes too much time to educate women on investing. That approach has serious issues and generally does not serve clients well.

Active portfolio managers at investment management firms charge investment management fees for portfolio management (i.e., active decisions about buying and selling stocks and managing risk). Analysts or stock pickers pitch their best stock ideas to the manager, who then later decides to buy the stock or pass. As someone who has been both an analyst and a portfolio manager, I know the dirty secret: Over the past 15 years, only about 37% of active stock fund managers have outperformed their designated benchmarks (like the S&P 500)[4] and just 29% of active US stock fund managers beat their benchmark after fees in 2019.[5] Jack R. Meyer, former president of Harvard Management Company, said it best: "The investment business is a giant scam. Most people think they can find managers who can outperform, but most people are wrong, I will say 85 to 90% of managers fail to match their benchmarks. Because managers have fees and incur transaction costs, you know that in the aggregate they are deleting value." What does this mean for you? Even if a portfolio manager or analyst tells you they can grow your money, there's no reliable guarantee that they'll actually be able to. And since their fees get paid whether your money grows or not, they have no real incentive to make sure you come out ahead. (There are certain types of advisors called fiduciaries, who are legally obligated to put your interests first, which we'll talk about later in this book, but not every advisor is one of these.)

4 Vanguard calculations, using data from Lipper, a Thomson Reuters Company. Based on funds' excess returns relative to their prospectus benchmark for the 15-year period ended March 31, 2020. Only funds with a minimum 15-year history were included in the comparison. Results for other periods will vary.
5 Fonda, Daren, *If You Still Own Actively Managed Stock Funds, Get Ready for Some Bad News. Barron's* Jan 23, 2020.

Moreover, most fund managers don't know who their clients are, which can create a disconnect between the portfolio manager and the person whose money they are managing. They don't think about the pensions of the firemen who are saving lives. They don't care if they are managing a college endowment for low-income kids to receive scholarships. They don't care about having a mission, nor are they connected with why they are in the business. They are wired for one purpose only: winning and investment performance. They don't really know their clients, nor do they connect their performance with impacting the lives of whose wealth they are managing. For you, this means that most male investment professionals will not ask you what is important to you nor give you credit for raising babies, managing a household, a career, and your wealth. Focusing on what you value long term might not align with their focus on short-term portfolio returns and gaining more assets under management. And since you're likely the only woman they're working with, your desire to align your values with your investing, or prioritize anything other than overall short-term portfolio return, will be incompatible with their echo chamber. At best, they will listen to you and then sell you what their boss told them to sell.

When I was a portfolio manager, I had the second-best performance out of 15 managers at the hedge fund I worked for in New York City. I loved working on Wall Street, and I was working my butt off and crushing it. During the year, no one except our general counsel ever told me how impressed everyone was with my work, my ability to develop a variant view and generate impressive risk-adjusted returns. My boss never asked me one question about my family or my future plans. He didn't care about me, and why should he? No one on Wall Street really cares about anyone on a personal level; the only thing that matters about a person is their money-making track record. But my differentiated investing style comes from a personal and diverse perspective, which I brought to the table and yet no one cared to ask me. You are only as good as your last trade. They don't care what your story is, what your core values are, and what you hope and dream.

This is the reason why a male financial advisor may not take the time to understand how to better serve you. Men value status, money, and power. Women value security, respect, and well-being. The abundance of male confidence and desire for money and power can actually lead to destructive investment behavior, as evidenced by a study conducted by the Warwick Business School, which surveyed 2,456 investors, 450 of which were female, between April 2012 and July 2016. The group of women outperformed the group of men in the study by about 1.2% per year because men trade more frequently than women, by 45%, which also results in higher transaction costs. Another study was done by Fidelity where over 8 million investment accounts were reviewed. Conclusion: Women earned higher returns and were better savers.[6]

A common practice is that an advisor might share a client's return on investment versus a standard benchmark like the S&P 500 (the index of 500 large companies listed on stock exchanges in the United States). When I talk to my male clients about market corrections, I talk about statistics and relative performance, just as other guys do. However, for some women like me, this isn't what I want out of an advisor or a portfolio manager boss. This type of relationship is solely based on performance, and that never worked well for me during my days in New York. I wanted an advisor who is focused on my long-term financial well-being and who can help guide me through the ups and downs of the

6 Michael Cannivet, Dec 29, 2018, "Why Women Are Better at Investing," *Forbes Magazine.*

market rather than talk about relative performance. Relative performance doesn't put food on the table.

While I was successful as a portfolio manager, my definition of success was not all about winning in the short term. I wanted to know who my clients were so I could connect what I was doing with whom I was investing for. Knowing their causes and values made me better at my job. And if my own boss had shared this same approach, I might have been able to thrive in my position rather than just barely surviving. He showed no interest in my long-term life goals and objectives and didn't know that I wanted to start my own firm one day. The stress of making it through each day without a supportive community wore me down over time. I was constantly nervous before the market opened at 9:30 A.M., weighed 97 pounds, and was losing hair by the handfuls. My body was so weak that I even had difficulty getting pregnant with a third child. In order to thrive, I had to leave this stressful life of taking a 5:50 A.M. train and not seeing my kids in the morning, and sometimes not seeing them all day. I wanted a relationship with my boss where we could celebrate my performance victories while at the same time have someone I could go to when I was dealing with personal challenges.

It became clear that was never going to happen, so I left the New York craziness and found a new job as a part-time consultant in New Canaan, Connecticut, the town I grew up in. During that same time, I had my third child. Life was good overall, but I felt like I wasn't taking the bull by the horn and didn't feel set for my future. I didn't have a clue what I wanted, and I was just waiting for things to get better in my career, the market, and my life. I later discovered I was missing a lot by avoiding putting myself first and not taking the time to figure out what was important to me. The truth is that, when it comes to money and investing, women want to connect, share our experiences, and feel supported. We want to use our wealth to be independent and to have the freedom to make choices about how we want to live. This puts women at a disadvantage when it comes to hiring a financial advisor and entering the investment world, since the rules of the road are different for us.

Look, I'm not saying all male advisors and analysts are sexist, bad at their job, out to take advantage of you, or even unqualified to help you build wealth. I've worked with many reliable, trustworthy men in the financial sector. But I am saying that the way that sector is set up does not give affluent women a fair chance to build wealth the way they want to because there just aren't enough women in that sector in the first place. It will take a long time to fix our financial system, but the glacial pace of that change should not prevent you from looking after your own self-interest. When I work with male investment clients, they love to hear about my performance as a portfolio manager at successful hedge funds in New York. When I work with women, they don't even care if I was a portfolio manager. I have learned I can most effectively help women invest by connecting with them, understanding their story, exploring their financial fears and vulnerabilities, and having a clear vision for how they want to use their wealth.

Okay, so male financial advisors aren't that into helping you build wealth on your terms. So just don't go to one, right? Male problem solved! Well, not quite. See, there are some other men who also might not be that into you managing and growing your own money, and these men are a bit harder to avoid. As much as I hate to do it, I have to bring up the husbands. The fantasy that your husband will take care of your financial future isn't just in your own head; pretty frequently it's also in his. Often the wives who want that fantasy end up married to husbands who want to control all the family's money, even when some or most of that money comes from the wife. One of my friends serves as a perfect example of what can go wrong with this mentality. She runs a very successful business, so I was shocked to find out that her husband rigidly controlled all of the money, both for the family and for her business. Even if she asked for account information about one of her big clients, he wouldn't give it to her. She was okay with this arrangement because that was how she had been raised. Her mother didn't know how much money the family had until her husband was on his deathbed, and even then, he didn't tell her himself; he told his son-in-law who told her. When I pointed out to my friend that she was putting herself in the same position as her mom by letting her husband control all of the money, she didn't care and was satisfied with trusting her husband. Now, they're getting divorced. Will she be able to take care of her financial future? I hope so, but she's certainly facing an uphill battle.

It can be easy for our husbands to convince us there is no reason for women to be engaged with the family's money or for us to convince ourselves that we don't need to think about our money at all. When times are good, husbands seem to have it all figured out while women are too busy working, taking care of the home, and managing kids' schedules to stop and ask questions. Making time to create a financial plan is nonexistent on the endless to-do list. And when times are not so good, our husbands still want us to think they have it all figured out even if they don't. What both advisors and husbands get wrong is that they don't start by asking what is important to you. If you are not participating in the planning process, how do you know if your dream can come true? Planning is the thing that helps us envision our dreams. Once we know what is important to you and what you want, putting a plan together is no longer a non-essential item that can be pushed to the back burner or ignored. Now, it's an essential task to do so that you can live your best life. You'll know whether an advisor or a husband is a keeper by how supportive they are of that plan.

In the next chapter, we'll talk more about the question of what is important to you and why that question is so hard to ask ourselves.

Chapter 3
WHAT WOMEN WANT

So now we know the two major impediments to women making their own financial plans: the myths about finances we've unwittingly embraced and the misaligned practices of the male-dominated finance world. To overcome those impediments and start taking control of our financial future, we need to pave our own path. The first step to moving in that direction is asking ourselves the fundamental question: What do I want?

Sometimes we might find ourselves in a similar position as Alice in Lewis Carroll's *Alice's Adventures in Wonderland* who, when coming to a fork in the road, asks the Cheshire Cat, "Would you tell me, please, which way I ought to go from here?" The Cheshire Cat responds, "That depends a good deal on where you want to get to." When Alice tells the cat that she "doesn't much care where," he aptly replies, "Then it doesn't matter which way you go."

LEWIS CARROLL

When I reached the fork in the road in my own life, I was lost just like Alice. I felt life was just passing by so quickly, and I was nowhere near where I thought I should have been by that point. Why couldn't I just pick a path?

At that point, I couldn't choose a path forward because they all seemed way too risky to me. I worried that whatever I tried to do with my money or my career would fail. I was so sick of dealing with the economic bubbles we had survived that all I wanted was the least-risky option. But when I paused for a moment to really evaluate my situation and what my financial future would look like if I stayed put, it quickly became clear that I would not be able to live for the next 40 years without either bringing in more income or investing. Visiting a hypothetical, let's say I'm single with my liquid net worth was about $2,000,000. If I was going to make that last for 40 years, my annual budget would be $50,000. To make that work, I would have to rent a really cheap apartment, my kids would have to share a bedroom, and I wouldn't be able to continue drinking my favorite $40 chardonnay (and not being able to drink Rombauer wine anymore really scared the shit out of me). This was not a financial plan; it was a plan for my withdrawal from life. What would my kids think of me if I moved them into the same type of shitty apartment my mom moved us into and made them live like I was raised? Did nothing I learned as a kid pay off?

When I would visit my grandma as a little girl, I remember her and my mom would oftentimes make fun of each other by calling themselves Gucci Bag Ladies. They would show each other their newly purchased Gucci luggage and handbags while joking that, if they ended up homeless, at least they would have their Gucci purses! Was I also going to become a Gucci Bag Lady, clutching my luxury handbags while I lived alone in my cheap apartment because I had been too scared to make a financial plan, which is the first step to make a dream life come true, when I had the chance?

The real question I needed to ask myself was: What did I actually want? My dream had been to start my own firm, so why had I buried my dreams? Far too few women ask themselves what they want and what happened to their dreams. We give up on our aspirations because we put our kids and other priorities ahead of our own. When our time becomes completely occupied with managing everything with the house and family, our goals and visions for our own lives get lost along the way. And maybe we don't take the time to understand what is important to us because no one has ever asked us. When was the last time someone asked you what you want (other than a waiter at a restaurant)?

Also, we're often too preoccupied with keeping what we have rather than thinking about what we might want instead. There is a phenomenon called loss aversion, where people would rather not lose money than make money. We have the same mentality with other aspects of life; we would rather not grow because there is risk in growth. By taking a risk and putting ourselves out there, we introduce too much and a new type of uncertainty and would prefer to just stay comfortable and keep tackling our daily to-do lists. We actually fear success. While I could have avoided loss through aversion and could have put my dreams of starting my own firm on pause in order to raise the kids, I instead did the opposite like any diva would do! I was so freaked out about my financial future and career failure that I felt like I had nothing to lose by doing what I did next. At least I would be remembered for being the Biggest Failure of the Class of 2001 Harvard Business School, if nothing else!

So how did I put aside my fear of being left behind? I wrote about it in the Harvard Business School reunion book for all my former classmates to read. We were asked to submit an update on what we have been doing since we graduated or since the last reunion. While the majority of folks usually brag about how successful they are, I decided to write about how unsuccessful I felt. Looking back on what I wrote makes me want to cringe, but I am also glad that I put it into words and shared it with others so I wouldn't forget my dreams.

> *"I'm at a very important pivot in my career since I graduated from HBS. After returning to investment banking after graduation, I discovered I loved working on the buy side and worked up the chain from analyst to portfolio manager at various investment management firms in NYC while having 3 kids (Alexandra age 9, Caroline age 7, and Henry age 3 ½), who are all a delight. When our family was relocated to Houston, I landed my dream job of continuing to work on the buy side at a firm in which I was to take over once my boss retired. However, I was not a good fit to the existing culture of the firm and the option to buy out my boss is no longer available to me.*
>
> *I am now at a crossroad in my career. I could just stay home and enjoy taking care of my 3 small kids, but I love what I do and want to continue to manage investments. I'm trying to embrace Oprah Winfrey's statement she made at the 2013 Harvard Commencement, 'Failure is just life trying to move us in another direction.' I therefore plan to start*

my own investment firm and possibly create a newsletter along with a book...I hope by the time we're at reunion I'll have figured out my new path in work and in life." May 2016

Throughout our lives, I think we come back to how we solved problems as kids and what those lessons taught us about ourselves. When I was trying to figure out what to do with my life, I had a flashback of helping my mother balance her checkbook. Back then, I never could have imagined how balancing checkbooks could lead to a career in finance where I could help people. When I worked on Wall Street, I spent many late nights building out financial models of companies, which allowed me to better service clients by making investment basics simple to understand. Financial modeling was such an important part of everything I did when I invested in companies. Then a thought popped into my head: What if I applied those same concepts to women and families and built financial and investment models to help them create a financial plan to achieve their goals and aspirations? And there was my answer.

"If we can find ways to become more comfortable with uncertainty, we can see the world more accurately and be better for it."

This quote is from the book called *Thinking in Bets*, written by Annie Duke.[7] But first, ask yourself: What have you not done yet that you know you'd regret never trying? When you put your busy life and your fear of loss aside, what do you really want to do? The thing I would regret not doing was starting my own financial firm to help women create secure financial futures for themselves. I thought of a book I had read recently, *Everything Is Figureoutable* by Marie Forleo, that told the story of Bronnie Ware, a nurse who cared for hundreds of patients during the final moments of their lives and who also wrote a book called *The Top Five Regrets of the Dying*. The most common regret they shared with Bronnie as they looked back on their lives was this:

"I wish I'd had the courage to live a life true to myself, not the life others expected of me."[8]

In the next few chapters, we'll get clear on the life you want to live that is true to you, and we'll start developing a financial plan that will get you there, starting with where you are today. Before you read on, consider what you would regret not doing in

---

7 Anne Duke, *Thinking in Bets*, (New York: Penguin Random House, 2018), page 47.
8 Marie Forleo, 2019, *Everything Is Figureoutable*, New York: Penguin Random House, page 247.

life. Imagine your doctor tells you that you have five to ten years to live. What would you do in the time you have left?

Chapter 4
WHEN LIFE GIVES YOU LULULEMONS

—◆◈—

S tock market investments are the essential tool
for wealth management, and what most women
don't realize is that they're actually the smarter sex
for investing. I have countless examples of times
when my perspective would have led to substantial
profit for our clients but was ignored by the men
I was working for and with, who were completely
out of touch with a significant data point in our
investment research: consumer behavior. Consumer
stocks' performance depends on the success of
the company, which is determined by whether
consumers spend money on their product or service.
And who spends the majority of the money in the
average household? Women do.

When we first moved to Houston, Texas, the oil and gas market was at an all-time high. Our fund had incredibly strong performance, and we didn't have to work very hard because the stocks did the work for us. But as a former commodities portfolio manager (someone who specializes in trading funds or stocks related to raw materials, like oil), I knew that the high volume of oil inventories would eventually lead to a downturn in the market, just like any other commodities market I had previously successfully invested in when I was a portfolio manager. It would be wise to start preparing for that eventuality as soon as possible. But my boss, as a former geologist, who was the main decision maker, was not concerned about it. Since he was knowledgeable about fracking—the technology that was responsible for growth in oil production and therefore the energy and production companies' stock prices—I assumed I also had no reason to worry. I wish I had listened to my gut because my instincts proved to be correct. In 2014, oil prices went from $100 per barrel to $35 per barrel, and our fund had invested heavily in oil-related stocks.

The silver lining with lower oil prices is that gasoline prices go down, which means that the average person has more money in their pocket to spend on consumer goods. I pushed my boss to pivot our investing approach to focus on consumer stocks. Based on what I knew about the latest brands and how women tended to spend their money, I was confident that Lululemon (a yoga clothing company) and TJ Maxx (a discount retail store with designer clothes and housewares) stocks would be a sound investment. I saw the women in my life spending their money at those stores and the brands seemed to be gaining popularity. I had a finger on the consumer pulse because I was a woman and had friends who were women, and I was paying attention to consumer behavior data points.

My boss turned down my proposal. He didn't understand the consumer. He didn't understand *women*. I felt that my hands were tied, that I couldn't invest in the stocks I wanted to. I wasn't in control. The fund had terrible performance, and we lost a lot of money. It was incredibly stressful to not be in a position to make my own decisions. I started to hate my job. All I wanted to do was to help make money for other people, but I had little control over how our fund was investing our clients' money. Why didn't I make a change, right then and there? In retrospect, I can see now that my ability to make strategic decisions was being hijacked by loss avoidance. I was making the classic mistake of maintaining the status quo in order to avoid risk of failure rather than taking a chance in order to achieve a greater reward. Ultimately, loss avoidance guarantees no profit and no dream life.

The truth is that not taking risks has its own risks. It takes a toll on your mental health and well-being. For me, I started to feel depressed and irritable. I found myself yelling at everyone around me, including random taxi drivers, and got stuck in a loop of negativity. I just couldn't see the positive side of anything anymore. Deep down, I knew what my dream was, but I was so committed to avoiding the risks, unsure of whether I could actually start my own firm, that it led to anxiety about the uncertainty of my future. If I didn't start my own firm, could I really live the rest of my life working for a fund where I had no control over the decisions that would determine how much money we made for our clients? Not fighting for your dream is the same as not taking risk and avoiding loss. Fighting for the life you want is about researching your why and developing a plan. The consequences of women accepting the status quo and making excuses to not take risks are profound: regret, death of our dreams, and loss of financial independence and security.

What can we do to manage the anxiety that comes with acknowledging that we need to take risks to secure the life that we want for ourselves? In a way, it's similar to going through the grieving process. There are five stages of grief: denial, anger, bargaining, depression, and acceptance. The most important stage is the final one. We have to accept that this is happening and figure out how to proceed. We have to figure out our own lives so that we're not dependent on someone else securing our financial future.

The problem is how do you know what your financial future should look like if you don't start with asking what is important to you? What are your priorities?

For women who would rather ignore this fundamental question and who don't want to take risks to grow their wealth through investing, they fail to realize that they are dangerously compounding negative effects. In the long run, this actually increases risk and can be downright dangerous. Compounding negativity is the fastest way to a deep, downward spiral. But compounding growth is the fastest way to catch your dreams and guarantee the life you want to live.

We might choose to not engage in our money because we are hijacked by loss avoidance. We simply don't want to lose what we already have. And what we might not be able to see is that there's always a risk, whether we make a change or choose not to make a change. We are always choosing whether to buy, hold, or sell a position in our lives. As a portfolio manager, I often had to make decisions about whether to buy, hold, or sell stocks I owned in my portfolio or potential new investment ideas. The goal was to generate a return, but that inherently required taking risks. The best way to minimize risk and to maximize return was to review each position and decide if I wanted to buy, hold, or sell more of each company's stock I owned. I based decisions on findings from my research, which included the company's performance, management's public comments, and my own financial models that evaluated the likelihood of a potential catalyst or market event that could affect the companies' stock performance.

While every company's competitive situation is different, each industry faces a variety of market threats and growth opportunities, which can engender situations that give investors opportunities to buy more stock, short (sell) the stock, or hold the position.

Buy. Some of my best investments resulted from me being confident enough to buy the stock of a company that I loved, such as Lululemon. Even though my fund did not invest in the consumer stock I had suggested, I made personal investments in Lululemon. In 2014, it was not a well-known brand, yet the stock was volatile as its growth trajectory was not stable yet. Anecdotally, all my friends were buying Lululemon clothing for their yoga classes but mostly to run errands. Then the stock got dumped and fell 30%, plummeting down to $40 per share. The company leadership had multiple missteps, including the scandal where certain pant styles were commonly being reported as see-through (and no one wants to be walking around in skin-tight leggings that everyone else but you realizes are see-through). Unfortunately, the founder and CEO found themselves in hot water for blaming the problem on the body shapes of some of its customers; they made a public statement that the pants were see-through because the women needed to buy a larger size. Obviously, telling women that it's their fault because of their body size did not go over well with the shareholders. However, I asked a lot of women if they had heard what the CEO had said and most had not, and they just continued to buy the clothes. Lululemon sought to restore its name with investors with a new CEO, who refocused the company on creating innovative products. I bought stock when the price dipped because I knew the problem was easy to fix and for the most part women were not aware of the problem. All the company needed to do was correct the manufacturing defect and get new leadership. I believed in Lululemon's long-term growth potential, and after they improved the clothing and brought on a new CEO, the stock price experienced substantial appreciation and made me a lot of money.

Sell. Sometimes the stock price correction is not a temporary dip or short-term price correction, and the price keeps going down due to company performance or market influences. This was the case when I analyzed Bed Bath & Beyond. I took the bet that the company would not continue to grow long term because I believed it could not compete against Amazon. For those who had invested in the stock early on in 2000 at $15 per share, selling it in 2015 when the stock was over $75 per share would have been a good idea. Since I didn't already hold the stock, I sold it short, which means I essentially borrowed shares from someone who owned it and made a profit by buying it back when the price dropped (a risky option since I could have lost money if the price increased). I wanted to bet on the company's continued decline because who needs Bed Bath & Beyond when we have HomeGoods (owned by TJ Maxx), Target, and Amazon? Now the stock is at $10 per share and I make money on my short.

Hold. While department stores were getting crushed over the last 10 years, I discovered TJ Maxx back in 2014. It was a company with something special that Amazon couldn't compete with. It's not a high-flier stock like Lululemon, but it's been a consistent performer. Shoppers go there regularly hunting for bargains and never leave the store empty-handed, which helps the company consistently grow. Holding on to this stock will pay consistent dividends over the long term.

Just like companies on the stock market, everyone's situation is different and every person is facing a variety of threats and opportunities. Life events can give us options to (a) buy and continue to grow, (b) sell and go away, or (b) hold our position. We can look at all the bad and disruptive things that happen in life as a stock price correction. It's easy to see how things out of our control—divorce, death, the economy, and even a pandemic—can set us back. But if we adopt a detached, objective perspective, we can analyze these setbacks and decide how to actively deal with them. Depending on your age and your financial position, you can decide to focus on things you can control and invest for growth, divest or sell to get out of a position, or hold for steady consistency. There are ways to figure out how periods of disruptions can eventually move us into recovery, growth, or retirement. Whether we are talking about the stock market or our personal lives, the cycles we go through personally and financially are similar.

> *"Everything comes to him who hustles while he waits."*
> *—Thomas A. Edison*

Buy. Are you thriving and generating amazing personal and financial returns like Lululemon? Investors all like a good growth story, and friends and family do, too! When a company is growing, they have clear plans and a long-term vision. The management team is excited to celebrate their successes with their investors on the quarterly conference calls. They share their financial update along with both opportunities and challenges and discuss how these steps fit into the company's long-term goals and mission.

Sell. Are you focused on just trying to survive like Bed Bath & Beyond? When a company is on the decline, the investor calls are usually depressing. The management teams are desperate to either find new growth opportunities or cut costs. Management teams are actually destroying capital and being wasteful with money. If an industry changes or is going through a major transformation, like Amazon disrupting traditional retail, can we retrain ourselves, figure out a new strategy, and pivot to a different direction?

Hold. Are you consistently growing while also staying true to what makes you a bit unique just like TJ Maxx? This, for most of us, is an ideal state of consistently growing and earning greater returns each year. Holding steady may be an appropriate path but only if the analysis underpins that decision.

In my midlife crisis, I went through all three of these phases. While I was once energized by picking stocks on a short-term basis and was trained well to do so, it no longer lit my fire. When I reached the end of my rope doing the same work at investment funds that I'd been doing for decades, it was time to sell and get out of there. My mental health and well-being were suffering, and it was clear I had to move on to something new. That's when I bought and invested in myself after reaching my low point, confident that I could grow my own value beyond what would have been possible if I'd stayed put. Now, I have established being unique and can now consistently help other women find their own steady financial growth while staying true to themselves.

In my life research stage phase, I found myself reflecting on times when I spoke to my clients in Houston and how they would ask me questions about a range of financial planning topics. These conversations opened my eyes to how people need advice, and I was challenged! I thought of the years I spent helping my mom with financial planning. How could I pivot and be of more value to clients, not just be a stock picker? I did my research and went to an industry conference called "Invest in Women." I started to understand I had to pivot by building my knowledge base, going back to school, and getting a certification to be a financial planner, which would allow me to combine financial planning with my investment knowledge. I listened to my inner voice and made the decision to invest in women, with women, *for* women.

In 2020, a report by McKinsey & Co, a US-based management consulting firm, titled "Women as the Next Wave of Growth in US Wealth Management" published their findings, which suggested that, over the next three to five years, women are expected to manage $30 trillion. The report also found that women value advisors and want to work with women.[9] At the same time, it also highlighted that women have lower self-confidence in their own financial decision-making and investment acumen. Why do women doubt their capability with finances when we know exactly what to do when it comes to something just as complicated and consequential: building a dream house? When you explore the idea of building a dream house, you already have a clear vision in your mind of exactly what it looks like. Similarly, when you explore the idea of a dream life, you have clarity on what you want that's very specific to you and the stage of life you are in. A dream life might be investing in a second home for family vacations, dedicating time to a nonprofit cause, starting a business, or even retirement.

---

9 Pooneh Baghai, et al., July 29, 2020, "Women as the Next Wave of Growth in US Wealth Management," McKinsey & Co.

The **Personal Investment Blueprint** is the simplified framework I created to help you achieve your life dreams by becoming financially literate and accessing risks in a low-cost way through active passive blend investing. And I'm here to assure you that you, as a woman, are inherently equipped to handle all four stages of the **Personal Investment Blueprint: Dream, Design, Hire, and Invest.** Just like when you build a house, you develop a dream vision, design a blueprint, hire experts, and invest in construction. This is the most direct pipeline to building a house as well as the most direct pipeline to generating personal and financial returns. This strategy will help you have clarity on where you are going, manage risks and financial choices with a financial plan, find trusted expert support, and invest your time and money in yourself and in the stock market, all with the goal of waking up each day excited to do what you love and feeling successful because you know where you are going and how to get there.

DREAM   DESIGN   HIRE   INVEST

We like to have certainty about our future. When we have more security in our dreams, we are happier and filled with the positive, strengthening, joyful, engaging, and fun energy. We are not stressed about things out of our control and we don't waste energy on complaining because we can focus on things we can control, which helps us stay focused and in command.

Personal Investment Blueprint

1. **Dream.** Figure out what you want. Be bold and push yourself as you explore a possible future version of your best life.
   - Lifestyle: vacation home, live-in help, sports car
   - Education: fund kids' educations
   - Legacy: leave money and maybe a business to your kids when you are gone
   - Entrepreneurship: start or join a business
   - Philanthropy: support charity causes or get really involved
   - Social Impact: invest your money to have social impact on society

2. **Design.** Put together your financial information.
   - Organize your incomes: recurring and variable
   - Map out expenses: essentials and flexible
   - Create your investment profile by putting together a balance sheet

3. **Hire.** Find a financial advisor who's a good fit for you.
   - Research and hire a trusted and competent financial advisor
   - Review your financial profile describing your income, spending patterns, current investment, and your dreams for the future
   - Build the financial plan that will take you where you want to go
   - Check in with your advisor quarterly to make sure you are on track
   - Remember that you have control and the ability to make changes

4. **Invest.** Execute your plan and invest with your financial advisor.
   - Instead of sitting in cash and letting your money decline in value, redirect your investment assets
   - Understand risks and be willing to take them
   - Let your assets compound so that you increase the likelihood of financial success
   - Focus your time and energy on what you want

Intentionality is everything. When someone knows where they are going, they have a clear direction. Investing in your dreams with genuine intent is not just a hope that everything will work out for the best; it is taking action toward the direction that offers a lifetime of benefits. Designing your dream life brings the kind of joy that comes from pursuing the path that brings you fullness, richness, and purpose. And when investing and figuring out your dream life actually makes *you* happy, it will also make everyone around you happy. Personal and financial investing isn't just good for you; it's good for the whole family.

Part Two

✖

DREAM, DESIGN, HIRE

Chapter 5

DREAM

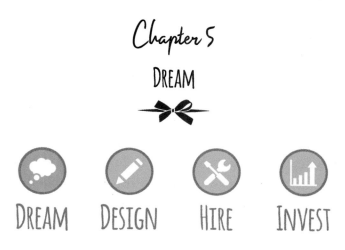

DREAM   DESIGN   HIRE   INVEST

"People get more inspired by purpose than money."
—Bill McDermott, CEO of ServiceNow

There is a difference between a goal and a dream. A goal is a number; usually it's a monetary goal guys want to hit and it's very specific. A dream is something bigger and longer lasting. What is your cause? What do you believe in? Why do you do what you do? Your dream is what you are betting will happen if your **Personal Investment Blueprint** is well developed.

One of the most important lessons I have ever learned about myself happened during my interview for Harvard Business School. After the very sweet admissions officer asked me a bunch of questions for which I had carefully prepared responses, she asked me one last question at the end of the interview: "If you didn't have to work, what would you do?" I told her I would be an artist because it's really hard to face a blank canvas and create something out of nothing. This was probably not an answer 99% of the people interviewed gave. Most guys would never think to give this answer, and most women would probably never feel that confident in giving such an answer. Harvard Business School is supposed to be churning out captains of industry, not artists!

At the young age of 26, I had a very clear five-year plan that didn't involve doing anything creative. Maybe the stress brought clarity to this hidden part of myself. Up to this point in my life, I had never had the opportunity to be creative, but my true inner self was already feeling like a caged animal in big corporate businesses, stifled in my pin-striped suits. Maybe I was hoping business school would help me figure out a way to be in business that would unleash my creativity so I would not have to be so confined and out of place. Sometimes we all need a blank canvas to help us focus on what we really want. The world gives us a lot of clutter we have to weed through. We don't all have to be artists, but we should all appreciate the freedom we have to create something with a purpose. To be creative entails taking risks. Not everyone will like what you create, but as long as it is true to who you are, and there is a story to your creation it doesn't really matter if anyone else likes it.

Now imagine a life where you don't have to work. You have enough money to take care of your needs, now and into the future. How would you live your life?

- What's the thing you've always wanted to do but have never had the chance to do?
- If you weren't doing what you're doing now, what would you be doing?
- When you were younger, what did you think you'd be doing now?
- What do you think you have the ability and skill to do but are holding yourself back from doing?

Connect the Dots

Investing allowed me to be creative. When I was analyzing and researching an industry and the companies in that industry, I would start by asking myself why someone would invest in this company. I was looking at how the company succeeds in its field compared to its competition, how the industry would perform in the future, which company might acquire who and for what reason, where the earnings can grow, and what multiple the market would be willing to pay for the company's earnings. What makes this company unique? Does the management team have a mission statement? What are their goals? How does the company expect to win? What are the risks of this company not succeeding? After doing my research, I would pull out a blank piece of paper and jot down relevant facts, figures, and impressions. Then I would look for patterns and ideas, mapping things out and connecting the dots. The more prepared I was, the more passionate I became with the investment. The more conviction I had, the larger position I would buy.

In much the same way, you have to paint the picture of where you think your "stock" can go by creating a vivid, detailed, descriptive vision of your future. You can only achieve what you can perceive. Women often don't get what they want because we don't ask for it. If you are not clear where you are going, you won't know you reached your dream life. The goal is to imagine yourself and your purpose three to five years in the future, and write down as many details as possible. Literally envision a specific date in the future, and imagine you are there. How old are you? What day of the week is it? Where do you live? How do you spend each hour of the day? Describe exactly what you see when you look out the window at your future self and your purposeful work. The more you can envision the future, the more likely it is to happen. Brian Scudamore, founder and CEO of 1-800-GOT-JUNK, built a $100 million business and credits his "painted picture" for his success. In fact, over 200 scientific studies have found that, as Scudamore says, "by visualizing abstract goals as pictures and videos, you're essentially turning your future into a story that will stick." In 2012, the National Institutes of Health found links between visualizing the future and success. In 2016, I created a picture of my future life and wrote in my Harvard Business School reunion update even though I wasn't sure that I would write a book and launch my own firm.

Years later, it's still eerie how much of what I wrote has come to be.

Now, let's get to the fun part—exploring your vision! I've created an exploration list to help get you started, but this is not meant to be all inclusive. Don't let me restrict what other opportunities or visions you might want for your own life. Sometimes we all need a blank canvas.

The Exploration List

Lifestyle

Have you ever traveled somewhere that felt so special that you thought, "Wow, I would love to have a home here where our family could come anytime we wanted!"? I had amazing memories as a kid in Nantucket. In the summers, my father would rent a house with his other single friends with kids, and I was in heaven. It was an escape from my life in New Canaan with my mother and a place where I could fit in with other kids whose parents were divorced. My dad wasn't wealthy enough to own a house there, but that would have been a dream of mine.

Find a photo of a home you love and put it somewhere you can see it every day, like the bathroom mirror or your phone screen saver. Imagine where the house is (on a beach, next to a lake, in a forest?), who is there with you (kids visiting on summer break, friends traveling to stay with you?), and how you spend your time there (making huge family dinners, reading by the lakeside?). Picture what kind of lifestyle you would like to have in your 60s and how you would like to spend your time. This is how to have clarity about your financial future. For me, I picture my kids grown up, coming to visit us at our second home in Old Greenwich, Connecticut, and talking about their plans about what they would like to achieve in life. This house should make your heart feel full.

- What childhood memories do you have that you would like for your family to experience?
- How do you want to spend your time together?
- Do you have enough money to support your lifestyle when you are older?
- If you could add one thing to your lifestyle that would get you closer to how you want to be living, what would it be?

Philanthropy

A very accomplished workaholic CEO who is a single mother with one daughter not only made her own wealth but also inherited a considerable sum of money from her family. Realizing she had more than enough money to support her frugal lifestyle now and well into her future and provide for her daughter's education, she was incredibly clear on her dream of starting a family foundation. Find a photo of organizations or people you are helping. Are you donating money to solve food challenges, address education disadvantages, or fund medical research? Are you giving back through leadership, donations, or organizing fundraising events? How is your money helping these people? Connect your actions with whom you are helping.

- How does giving represent values for you (and your family)?
- What is important for you to accomplish with your philanthropy?
- Have you or someone important in your life been affected by something profound, like cancer, food insecurity, or domestic violence?
  - » How can you contribute to those organizations to help support their cause?
  - » Or, if there is a lack of existing resources, could you start an organization?

Legacy

When my middle child, Caroline, was young, she told me that she missed me when I was gone at work and asked me why I had to work outside the home. I told her that work makes me happy and fulfilled. Now, work means much more to me because I see it as a legacy I will leave to my children. Having learned nothing about money and investing from my mom put me at a huge disadvantage when it came to figuring out what to do with my life. I'm building a business to help women invest their money so they can live their dream life and not run out of money; I also want to build a legacy of inclusivity and community that will be passed on to my kids. If you want to leave a legacy for your kids, find a photo of them and place it somewhere you will see it often. Or if you want to leave legacy to an organization, find a photo of the organization or people who are positively impacted by the organization's work.

- What do you want to be remembered for?
- If your children's children could read your history, what would it say?
- Who or what was the greatest influence on you in developing your principles?
- What did you learn from your parents? What do you wish you would have learned?
- What do you want to pass on to your children?

Entrepreneurship

As a 13-year-old, my oldest daughter, Alexandra, loved visiting a coffee shop in Jackson Hole called Persephone Bakery. We loved the coffee, bread, and décor. It was our happy place as soon as we landed in Wyoming. Alexandra loved the bakery so much that she has often talked about starting her own coffee shop some day. I love that my daughter has dreams of starting her own business from an early age, and I hope more and more women will embrace any dreams they have of being entrepreneurs. Not only do women-owned businesses fuel the economy and represent 42% of all businesses, but they are growing at twice the rate of businesses owned by men.[10] Women-owned

10 This 2019 State of Women-Owned Businesses Report, commissioned by

businesses total nearly 13 million, employing 9.4 million people and generating $1.9 trillion of revenue. Entrepreneurship allows women to have flexibility and freedom and provides an avenue for solving creative problems.

- Is there something you wish existed but could never find?
- Is there a particular need that you have noticed in people around you?
- Do you have expertise in a subject that you would love to explore with a publication or as a consultant or advisor?
- Do you want to improve an existing product or service?

Woman-Owned Businesses Are Growing 2x Faster On Average Than All Businesses Nationwide

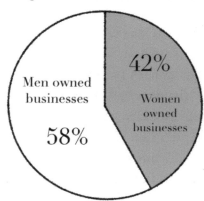

American Express is based on data from the United States Census Bureau Survey of Business Owners (SBO).

Education

Paying for college these days is a lot more expensive than it used to be. Tuition inflation is running between 5% to 7% per year, which is more than twice the rate of inflation. Public universities cost on average $26,000 per year, and the average private college charges twice that. Most families use a combination of 529 plans, student loans, scholarships, and grants.[11] A good friend of mine took a few years off of work to raise her kids. Private school was one of her dreams for her three boys, but her husband didn't want to pay the tuition. So she went back to work; not only does she love her job, but she pays for all three kids to attend one of the best private schools in the country, which provides her with a deep sense of meaning and purpose.

Maybe you're interested in pursuing your own education. Fortunately, there are plenty of avenues for gaining expertise in a field that interests you. One of my friends serves as an inspirational success story for continuing her education later in life. She had worked at a nonprofit before she got married and had kids. While raising her three children, she developed an interest in nutrition. When someone

---

11 A 529 plan is a tax-advantaged investment vehicle in the US designed to encourage saving for the future higher education expenses of a designated beneficiary.

suggested she could start a career as a nutritionist, she enrolled in online classes and completed her college coursework at night. It took four years to get another degree, but she did it!

- What is the most important thing education has provided for you?
- What role does education play for future generations?
- If you could be an expert in something, what would it be?
- How are you going about educating your children and grandchildren on your wealth?

Social Impact

Social impact investing refers to investments made into companies, organizations, and funds with the intention to generate a measurable, beneficial social or environmental impact alongside a financial return. Impact investments provide capital to address social or environmental issues. As an investor, you can either have your investment portfolio geared towards social impact or you can be part of organizations that address the cause you are interested in.

- Where are the areas that you want to have impact?
- When you consider your investments, what significance does making an impact have, and what does that look like?

Priorities

Once you start dreaming about the possibilities for your future, you may become overwhelmed with all the desires you have unleashed. It will be necessary to evaluate and prioritize your dream options in order to be effective in achieving your most important dream. When I set my priorities, I selected two areas of focus: legacy and lifestyle. I prioritized legacy because after being laser focused on managing money as a portfolio manager, I wanted to make more of a contribution. I did some soul searching to find how I could have more of a lasting impact. I realized I could help women by teaching them about wealth management and addressing women's needs that most male financial advisors ignore. I also prioritized lifestyle because I want to make sure our family can always take vacations and create experiences together. We have taken European vacations every year, even when the children were very young, and they grew tremendously from these experiences. We always look forward to the next vacation.

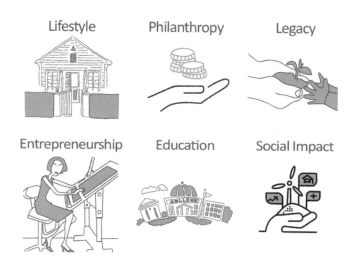

Lifestyle   Philanthropy   Legacy

Entrepreneurship   Education   Social Impact

The more conviction you have about what you want in life, the more focused and passionate you will become in wanting to invest in this idea. Connecting your money with your why is very similar to researching a company and modeling out the financials to see if it is a good investment.

Bottom line: Your vision for your future is not about how much money you have or don't have. It's about how much clarity you have in knowing what you want to achieve, how confident you are in communicating your goals, and connecting with your money to help you achieve your goals.

Chapter 6
DESIGN

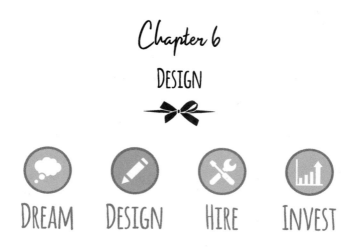

DREAM   DESIGN   HIRE   INVEST

When you build a house, you start to create a vision of what it will look like by driving through neighborhoods or browsing architectural books. You find a good contractor and architect by asking for referrals from friends. You talk to other people who have built homes to learn from the mistakes they've made and the things they ended up loving about their new home. You put together a budget, commit to a construction team and schedule, and then you break ground and start to build. All of your energy and focus is on managing the build of your dream house. If you skip any of these steps, you run the risk of building a house that isn't structurally sound or doesn't fit with what you really want.

Now that we have painted the picture of your success, it's time to design the financial plan that helps enable you to get what you want.

Unfortunately, a dream without a financial plan is just a wish.

Just like you can't build a house without an architectural plan, you can't achieve your dream without a financial plan. Money often feels like an emotional thing, but it doesn't have to be. You just need to gain clarity and confidence in your family's financial future. In order to do that, you need to sit down and get your money organized. You are in control. This leads us to a simple method of managing money that has to do with choosing how much you save, how much you spend, and how long you work in the first place.

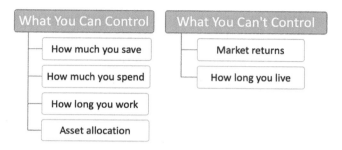

So now let's get ready to design your financial plan to create your future dream life. A financial plan boils down to where you are right now, where you want to be, when you want to get there, and how you plan to make that dream into a reality. Imagine that you are the family's Chief Financial Officer (CFO) because you are in fact the main breadwinner, or you and your spouse both decided it was in the family's best interest for you to be the main decision maker. A good CFO is not just a bean counter; they are very strategic in planning finances and making sure the family is on track and managing its resources well. This process can also help you become more sensitive to where all your money goes and how quickly things add up.

About two months before we left for a big European vacation, my husband was traveling a lot for work. This meant that I was taking the kids out to dinner often to avoid having to clean up dinner messes on top of everything else I was managing at home by myself. The girls wanted to buy clothes for the upcoming trip, but I made a deal with them: If we stopped eating out for a few weeks and decided to forgo shopping, we could save money to go shopping in Paris (and who wouldn't rather shop in Paris!). We saved $2,500 for our Paris shopping and dining, and it was so much more delicious eating escargot and mussels, my girls' favorite hors d'oeuvres in France.

Planning helps us make decisions in the present while simultaneously thinking about the impact of these decisions on our future.

We are going through this design (financial plan) process because we need to make sure you have enough cash to weather the storms (the ups and down of life and the stock market) and invest your money so you can achieve your future dream. Let's start by organizing spending categories into buckets and thinking about where your money tends to go and why. That way, you have more power over your money, better understand your family's income, and start putting your money towards your financial dreams. Keep these tips in mind as you work through your own financial plan:

- Setting small goals allows for more frequent wins. This process of putting together a family cash flow statement and balance sheet might seem overwhelming, so break it down into small parts.
- Reaching these small goals keeps you motivated. Set a timer and just do one part at a time.
- Staying motivated helps you crush more goals. Try to tie some small reward after you put forth this work. Take a nice bath, get your nails done, go for a nice walk, or enjoy a nice glass of wine!

Income Statements

An income statement allows you to strike a balance between what you earn (income) and what you spend (expenses). If these two categories don't align and your expenses exceed your income, you could encounter cash-flow problems, run through your savings, or start accumulating debt. Think of your savings pouring into a pot annually, like a river flowing into a reservoir.

This reservoir collects the savings, which increases the water level (the balance sheet), which gets bigger by the annual savings. This pond of savings will continue to help fuel your growth to your dreams.

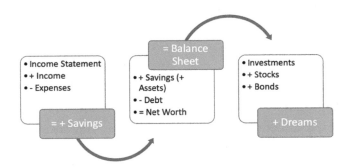

In sum, spend less than what you make and invest the rest. While this sounds simple, plenty of women never take the time to understand the income and expenses of their own family finances. Back before the financial crisis, the hedge fund industry and active management of money was once a huge wealth creator for portfolio managers. As Warren Buffett once wrote, "When trillions of dollars are managed by Wall Streeters charging high fees, it will usually be the managers who reap outsize profits, not the clients." When the financial crisis happened, the hedge funds weren't able to protect their investors as much on the downside as they had promised, so the hedge fund managers lost money. Investors no longer wanted to pay high fees for hedge fund performance, and high fees were declining. Many hedge funds shut down, and those families' incomes went to zero. Because the wives of these hedge fund managers did not understand (or did not accept) that their husband's income had decreased and therefore their expenses needed to decrease, they refused to scale back their spending on nonessentials. As you can imagine, situations like this led to high levels of stress and strain and often ended in divorce.

Here's how you can arm yourself with knowledge about your family's income and expenses:

1. As my family's Chief Financial Officer, I've already done the hard work for you by

creating a spreadsheet you can download, for free.[12] Go to www.wealthengagement. com/bundles.

2. Go to the Income Statement tab.

3. Don't forget to copy and paste your dream at the top of the spreadsheet so you don't lose sight of your long-term vision.

4. Figure out what your family's income is each month after tax. Put this amount in the income section.

5. List all your monthly expenses. Review your bank statements and credit card bills, remember to account for items that you paid for with cash.

Having this knowledge will help you decide what to spend today, this month, and this year. Rather than make a series of ad hoc decisions, you can weigh all your needs and desires against your income and set priorities. Start by identifying your essential expenses, such as a mortgage, loan payments, utilities, transportation, health care, and insurance premiums. If you have credit card debt, you must be paying this off monthly, so the only debt you should have (if any) is a mortgage. Then identify

---

12 I provided spending categories we use and have simplified the spreadsheet to make it accessible to anyone and everyone. However, please personalize it and figure out what works best for you.

your flexible expenses and divide them into must-haves (food and clothes) and nice-to-haves (eating out, entertainment, travel, and more clothes). If you must cut back, flexible expenses that are nice-to-have are a good place to start, although you may also have to manage essential expenses. Could you move to less expensive accommodations or lease a less expensive car? Monitor your spending for a couple of months and revise your budget as needed. Chances are you'll find that you forgot some expenses and that you need to adjust some spending across categories.

Here is a simple diagram to follow to better manage your spending. Every time you make a purchase decision, check your mental box which category it goes into. The basic rule of thumb is known as the 20/30/50 rule. Start with your after-tax income. Save 20% of your after-tax income, which goes towards **Dreams**—retirement, second home. You aim to limit your **Essential** expenses to 50% of that after-tax figure, and your **Flexibles (Wants)** consume 30% of your after-tax pay.

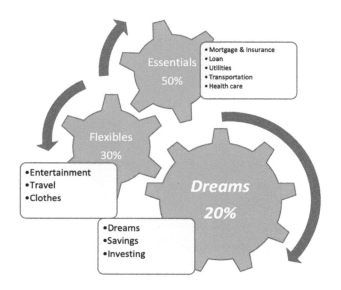

To achieve financial independence and minimize the chances of disaster, you need to get rid of consumer debt, save for retirement (including funding your dreams), and build your emergency fund. Limit your essentials to 50% of after-tax income. You may have to trim some of your expenses, which might take a while. You may be discouraged by how far you are from the ideal, but running the numbers can help you understand why your money isn't working for you.

Why is it so important to keep your **Essential** expenses at 50% of your after-tax limit?

- **It gives you flexibility.** If your income drops by half, you will still be able to pay your essential bills.
- **It helps you figure out what you can and can't afford.** If you're considering adding a loan payment or other contractual obligations to your expenses, you simply check to see if it would push you over the 50% mark. If not, you can consider adding the payment.
- **It gives you balance.** Limiting your essentials allows you to have money for the pleasures in life, such as eating out and vacations, without stress.
- **Save for tomorrow.** If you are spending more than 80% of your after tax income to support your current lifestyle, then you are taking away from your future self and your ability to achieve your dream.

A podcast I listened to told the story of a woman who had worked as a housekeeper and managed to take a trip around the world after her seventh kid (yes, seventh!) went off to college. How did she manage to save enough money to do this after raising seven kids on a housekeeper's salary? No matter how hard things got, she would put $5 away in a coffee can every day. She stayed focused on her dream to travel the world without sacrificing any of the family's essentials.

"Do not save what is left after spending, but spend what is left after saving."
—Warren Buffett

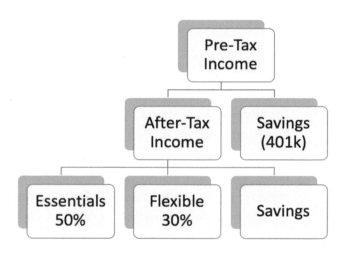

It makes sense that women might be nervous about their financial future if the husbands typically manage investments and review credit cards, leaving us with a lack of control over our finances once we leave the workplace. We just need to get ahead of the numbers and learn to engage in our family's wealth. We may be intimidated by the idea of investing or learning about money because it seems too complex (and who has time to squeeze in reading a book on investing on top of everything else?). But I guarantee that, as long as you can do simple arithmetic and learn a handful of new vocabulary words, you have all the tools you need to take control of your family's finances.

Balance Sheets

The next part of your financial plan is to include your family's balance sheet, which is a snapshot of everything you own (assets) and owe (liabilities).

The balance sheet either grows by the amount of savings you earn or decreases by the amount of debt you are accumulating.

Assets can be anything of value: cash, house, investments, insurance policies, cars, retirement accounts, and college funds. Liabilities include debt obligations, student loans, credit card debt, and mortgages. A balance sheet, as the name suggests, always has to balance what you own versus what you owe at a point in time. Taking the difference between your assets and your liabilities shows your family's equity (or net worth) and helps you see if you are in good financial health. Other institutions, like banks, will decide whether they should lend you money based on this evaluation. A balance sheet also can show you whether your family has the resources needed to meet its future obligations.

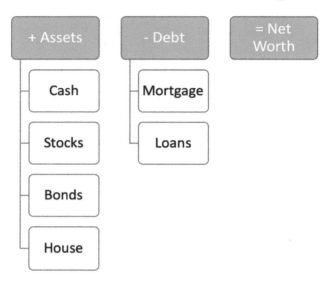

Let's say a house (asset) is worth $1,000,000, but you have an $800,000 mortgage loan (liability) on the house. This means the equity (worth) you have in the home is $200,000. If you sold the house today and the seller paid you $1,000,000 to purchase your house, the mortgage bank collects on their $800,000 mortgage loan and you receive $200,000 (the equity left on the house) in cash or wired to your bank.

Mind the Gaps

We start off in our careers and lives earning and spending money, working and playing hard. When we are in our 20s, we want to establish ourselves in our careers and possibly start to settle down with a spouse and kids. Once kids are in the picture, we need to buy a house and start planning for all the future obligations, like college funds. And, for some, we start to spend a certain amount of money, which locks us into a certain lifestyle that's hard to change down the road. My dad, who spent his entire career in sales and marketing, once let me in on an insider secret that management encourages sales guys to buy expensive things, so they get locked into an expensive lifestyle and won't have a choice but to make their sales numbers. This is the money trap. Whether you're in sales or not, when you start making a lot of money, you don't realize the "golden handcuffs" that come with this money once you start to enjoy spending it on expensive things. Money is complex. Wealth is both emotional and logical. Even wealthy people are just as likely as anyone else to mess up their finances because it doesn't matter how much money you make if your burn rate exceeds your income.

Here are some ways to avoid the golden handcuffs and keep your lifestyle to a manageable level:

- Think of clothes as investments and only purchase clothing items you plan to wear at least twice a month. About half of Americans say emotions drive them to overspend when they're shopping, and I would bet we only wear 20% of the clothes that are in our closets.
- Consider how much you spend on coffee and alcohol each month and experiment with ways to cut back on this by changing the type of beverage you buy or how often you buy it. Spending $5 on a latte every day adds up to almost $2,000 over the course of the year!
- Give your kids a spending budget on clothes and let them manage the tradeoffs on price and quantity of clothes.
- Share your goals with your spouse and your kids so you can make decisions together, like not eating out for a month to save up for a shopping trip in Europe.

Emergency Fund

When everyone else is selling their stocks during a correction, money you keep aside gives you piece of mind so you don't have to react when everyone else is reacting. But first you need to figure out how much money to set aside. This money is typically called an emergency fund. Some advisors suggest you put aside six months' worth of essential expenses, but we really need this money to last you the duration of a potential recession, which typically runs for 24 months. The money is not meant to be invested unless you are really daring and have a secure job; you can then take advantage of zigging when others are zagging and you can use any cash you have on the sidelines to buy but for the rest of us it's there so you can sleep well at night if you lose your job. With our rule of thumb where we budget 20% for savings, 30% for flexible expense, and 50% essential expenses, we need to make sure if your income were to go to zero, you would have at least a year to support your essential expenses. To keep numbers really simple, let's say you make $200,000 annually after tax, so 50% of your income supports your **Essential expenses**. You should have $100,000 sitting in cash on the sidelines in case you lose your job, which is 12 months of essential expenses (or to be very conservative, have $200,000 in cash in case it takes two years to find a new job). You definitely don't want to make a bad short-term decision like sell your stock portfolio to support your lifestyle.

What Can Go Wrong Without a Financial Plan

Allison is a 55-year-old divorcée. She hasn't worked since she started having kids, who are now grown and are no longer dependents. She has an amazingly strong balance sheet with $10 million as her liquid net worth. She also lives a very extravagant lifestyle. The question is: Will Allison be okay?

To evaluate this, we need to examine her financial behavior. Allison anticipates spending $720,000 per year to sustain her extravagant lifestyle. With not investing her money and earning 0% return, she will run out of money in 13 years. However, if Allison would invest her $10 million in 100% in equities at that rate of spending, Allison will run out of her $10 million base of assets in around 21 years unless her investment returns are greater than 10% every year and there is never a market correction (a very aggressive and risky return target).[13] In other words, her portfolio would have to add $1,000,000 of after-tax gains and the portfolio would need to never have a drawdown, which is unlikely over a 30-year time horizon.

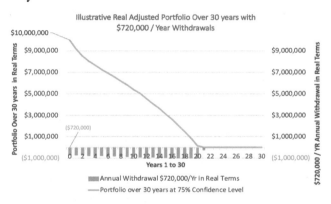

Illustrative Real Adjusted Portfolio Over 30 years with $720,000 / Year Withdrawals

---

13 Source: Portfolio Visualizer. Assumptions: Monte Carlo simulation results for 10,000 portfolios with $10,000,000 initial portfolio balance using available historical returns data from Jan 1994 to Dec 2019. The historical return for the selected portfolio for this period was 11.35% mean return (9.73% CAGR) with 14.36% standard deviation of annual returns. The simulation results are based on generated nominal returns and specified inflation adjusted withdrawals ($720,000 per year). The simulated inflation model used historical inflation with 2.21% mean and 1.17% standard deviation based on the Consumer Price Index (CPI-U) data from Jan 1994 to Dec 2019. The generated inflation samples were correlated with simulated asset returns based on historical correlations. The available historical data for the simulation inputs was constrained by SPDR S&P 500 ETF Trust (SPY) [Feb 1993–Jul 2020].

If spending a lot on clothes gets in the way of her having money in the long run, then she can safely spend only $360,000 a year, which is a major change from her current spending profile. Her spending levels maybe complex and emotional (for example, she may be spending most of her money on maintaining an old estate she grew up in and needs to let go of it). She just needs some planning advice. At least she now knows she has control and can make better short-term decisions. She knows that those short-term decisions have long-term repercussions on her ability to achieve her dreams, which in her case is lifestyle.

You can start to evaluate who you want to be over a longer time so that you are not making short-term decisions that you might regret later in your life. You now have a financial plan, you know what you want, and you won't run out of money because you can see with better clarity your financial future.

Putting It All Together

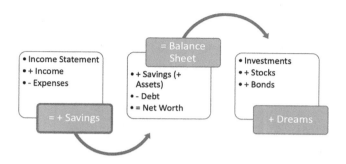

As you spend (expenses) less than you make (income), this annual savings flows to your balance sheet, which is the snapshot of everything you own (assets) and owe (debts) and adds to your net worth when your assets grow by the amount of savings you contribute or by the amount of the debt you pay off. Your liquid assets (cash as one example) then gets invested in your portfolio, which flows into growth assets. This really should look like a beautiful stream of water, like a river constantly flowing and growing. The more you invest for your future, the faster you can see the water from your beach house you want to buy!

Investment professionals can project out your income statement and your balance sheet and take a look at what your financial future will look like in 10 years, 15 years, or any other time frame you care to review and they figure out how much your dreams will cost, how long it will take to save for your dreams, and how to approach success using different asset associations and market performances. The forecasting model based on probabilistic and historical return data built by Portfolio Visualizer helps us quickly figure out where the gaps are. Do you need to make more money, spend less money, or have a more aggressive asset allocation towards stocks to reach your goals? These three drivers are what you can control in your life!

$$Chapter\ 7$$

HIRE

DREAM   DESIGN   HIRE   INVEST

There are folks who can build and design a financial plan and investment portfolio all on their own, just as there are some rare individuals who can build and design a house all on their own. In fact, this book's purpose is to show you how you can design a financial plan and invest your wealth all on your own, which we will discuss more in the next chapter. But even the best doctors won't perform surgery on their own loved ones out of fear they might make a mistake by letting emotions influence their performance. Financial advisors help you navigate the market when it gets volatile and help adjust your plan when life changes. Most importantly, they are there to help you when you are under stress and prone to making mistakes and bad decisions. Having a financial advisor who has years of knowledge and experience is tremendously valuable.

Women are more likely to seek an advisor after a major life event, such as a marriage, major inheritance, divorce, or loss of a loved one. Women often experience greater financial impacts from divorce or separation than men and are twice as likely as men to cite divorce as the reason for opening a new investment account. The dissolution of a marriage is an even more powerful driver of switching financial advisors than the loss of a loved one. To address the unique needs of women divorcées, some firms and advisors have built successful specialty service offerings by creating a compelling value proposition for women undergoing divorce and helping to chart a course towards financial independence.

Even though I'm an experienced financial advisor and an investor, I have never launched a business before. I was nervous, eager to get going, anxious about my big change, stressed about money, and worried about making the right decision. So when it was time to start my own business venture, I hired professional business coaches who met with me regularly to discuss my plan and to help me develop my why and clarify my core values. We designed my five-year dream plan, and then we broke that plan down into a three-year plan, one-year plan, and 90-day plan. My coaches help me stay on track with my business and help me with strategy and structure in much the same way a financial advisor does with wealth management. Hiring the right advisor can help you have a better chance of success to go where you want to go.

The Hiring Decision

Finding the right advisor is key to making sure your interests are aligned. Let's look at some key considerations that will help you find an advisor who is the right fit for you.

Initial Meeting. The initial assessment should include an examination of other financial management topics, such as insurance and taxes. The advisor needs to be aware of your current estate plan (or lack thereof) as well as other professionals on your planning team, such as accountants and lawyers. If you are married or have a life partner, you should bring them along to the meeting or have a very good reason why you prefer not to.

Certification. An advisor doesn't need to be a CERTIFIED FINANCIAL PLANNER™, or CFP® Professional, but it would be great if he or she is one. The fact that they have the certification means they care enough about their clients to have gone through a two-year process with continuing education requirements.

Fees. You should be told up front how, and how much, a potential advisor will be paid. You shouldn't have to ask. The correct method of payment is by fee only. Fee-only financial advisors do not get paid commissions. Their only objective is to provide sound financial advice to the client, who is paying them an hourly fee, flat retainer fee, or asset under management fee. The advisor needs to explain fees to you simply on a piece of paper. If the advisor is investing in mutual funds, there is an investment management fee associated with mutual funds that might not be disclosed to you unless you know to ask. An advisor should never ask you to write a check to him or her. You should write checks only to a brokerage firm, an insurance company, or another financial services firm.

Consistency. Your advisor should be calling you in down markets as well as in up markets. You should hear from them at least every 12 months.

Fiduciary. A fiduciary is defined by the legal and ethical requirement to put your best interest before their own. Does your potential advisor have other businesses that may lead to a conflict of interest, such as investment banking, insurance, or lending? It's important to know ahead of time and take the conflicts of interest into account before entering into a professional relationship with them.

Personalization. Does your advisor start talking about their track record as an investor or do they ask you what is important to you? A good financial advisor will ask you questions like:

- How is your health?
- Are you in debt?
- Are you responsible for aging parents?
- Do you have a will or trust?
- Will you inherit money someday?
- Do you need to make a major purchase, like a new house?

- Do you have a retirement plan?
- Do you have adequate insurance?
- Are you saving for your children's education?
- What are your long-term goals and priorities?

It can be difficult to find an advisor who has all of the above qualities and is also a good personality fit. Ask for referrals from your friends or ask your CPA or your trust and estates lawyer for a recommendation. Meet with as many advisors as you need to until you find a good fit.

14 Terms To Know Before You Sit Down with an Advisor

Stock Market. Stocks are bought and sold throughout the day on a stock exchange, like the National Association of Securities Dealers Automated Quotation system (Nasdaq) or the New York Stock Exchange (NYSE), and their prices can fluctuate greatly depending on such factors as how much money the company makes, news stories, and the overall health of the general economy. Investors can buy shares in an individual company stock, or they can buy a slice of a pool of stocks alongside other investors.

Here's the basic process:

- You invest by buying an ownership stake in a company (when you buy a share in an IPO, the money goes directly to the company).
- The company uses that money to invest in selling more products or services.
- The equity you purchased is now worth more, so you can sell it to someone else for a profit.

Stocks or Equities. When someone buys a stock, they are buying a portion of a company, and they become an owner of that company. Most stocks have hundreds or thousands of owners, and typically investors own a tiny fraction of a company. When you buy a stock, the price you pay is subject to how well the company is run and how much money (profit) it makes. Stock investors participate in a share of the company's profits, paid through dividends (a quarterly cash payment) and capital appreciation (growth in the stock's price).

Bonds. Bonds are loans. When you buy a bond, you become a lender to the entity that issued the bond. Most bonds pay you interest. Your loan lasts for a certain period of time until the date when the bond reaches maturity. As long as the institution does not go bankrupt, you will get your principal back on the bond but no more than the principal on the bond. Bonds do not typically trade on exchanges, but you can still buy or sell them from brokerages. There are many types of bonds but the main ones are government bonds, municipal bonds, and corporate bonds. US government bonds (also known as T-bills or treasuries) are issued and guaranteed by the US government. Municipal bonds ("munis") are debt securities issued by state and local governments. These can be thought of as loans that investors make to local governments and are used to fund public works such as parks, libraries, bridges, roads, and other infrastructure. Corporate bonds are debt securities issued by companies.

Alternatives. Alternative investments can include real estate, hedge funds, private equity, and commodities such as gold. With real estate, you may earn a return when your tenants pay rent.

Asset Allocation. Asset allocation can be visually represented with a pie chart, where each slice of the pie represents a percentage of each particular asset class, such as stocks, bonds, cash, and alternatives. When folks talk about asset allocation, they are usually talking about their investment account.

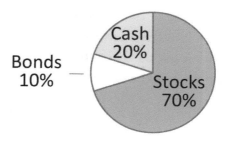

Compound Growth and Interest. Compounding growth is when you earn more money on money you invested. As Benjamin Franklin succinctly described it, "Money makes money. And the money that money makes, makes money." When you save or invest, your money grows when you earn interest on interest (or pay interest on interest). For example, let's say you put $1,000 in the bank and your bank pays you 1% interest per year. You earn $10 on the $1,000 at the end of the first year. The starting total for the following year will be $1,010, which means that you will add 1% of $1,010 (or $10.10) the following year. The starting total and amount added will increase each year.

Investing in publicly traded companies allows you to participate in a company's growth. Growth usually compounds, and investing in companies allows you to put your money to work with the expectation of earning a return. The spirit of entrepreneurship, population growth, and advancements in technology means the US economy over the long run will go up, and therefore the stock market will also go up.

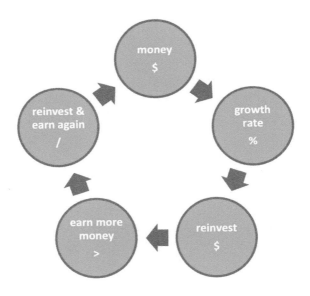

Diversification. Diversification is the practice of spreading money among different asset classes and geographic regions to reduce risk. It's a risk management technique that spreads your bets so that you are not putting all of your eggs in one basket.

- Risk Reduction: While you can't eliminate risk completely, you can manage your level of risk by allocating to different types of assets. If one investment performs poorly, other investments may perform better over the same time period.
- Capital Preservation: By reducing the likelihood of steep drawdowns, diversification can make it much easier for an investor to protect their capital.
- Hedging Potential: Diversification can help a portfolio grow both when markets boom and when returns are muted in one sector. It gives an investor the chance to achieve positive returns in one market when another market is generating negative returns.

Benchmark. A benchmark is a standard against which the performance of a security, mutual fund, or investment manager can be measured. For example, the S&P 500 index, a popular benchmark, has underperformed Alphabet Class A shares (Google) by 19% year over year. In other words, Google has outperformed the S&P 500 benchmark by 19% year over year.[14]

---

14 Source: Nasdaq.com as of 8/28/2020. Powered by EdgerOnline ©2019, EDGAR®Online, a division of Donnelley Financial Solutions. EDGAR® is a federally registered trademark of the US Securities and Exchange Commission. EDGAR Online is not affiliated with or approved by the US Securities and Exchange Commission.

Google vs S&P 500 Year over Year Relative Return

Mutual Fund. A mutual fund is a pooled investment vehicle, meaning many investors "pool" their money together in a single fund. Mutual funds hold a basket of many different securities, allowing fund holders to buy into the pool, instantly gaining exposure to lots of stocks more cheaply than owning each stock outright and diversifying the risk of only owning a single stock. Unlike when an investor buys shares of an individual company, however, when buying into a mutual fund, the individual investor does not decide which individual stocks are held in the basket. This basket of securities is managed by a professional money manager who can either (a) passively track an index, which is a basket of securities that represent the broad market it attempts to replicate, or (b) actively choose individual securities.

Index Fund. An index fund is a low-cost fund designed to mirror the performance of a specific market index, such as the S&P 500. Index funds are considered to be passively managed because the portfolio manager of each index fund is replicating the index. Expenses of index funds tend to be lower than mutual funds because the manager is not actively researching, buying, and selling securities.

Exchange Traded Fund (ETF). An exchange traded fund is similar to a mutual fund in that it invests in a basket of securities. However, they generally passively follow an index, although there are a few actively managed ETFs. And unlike a mutual fund, which trades only once a day, ETFs trade on a stock exchange throughout the day, so investors can buy or sell at any time, just like a stock. This intraday trading allows investors to know the price of their investment at any point in time, whereas mutual fund prices are only known after the market closes for the day. ETFs are tax efficient and have no minimums.

Active Management. Active management is a portfolio management strategy where the fund manager chooses specific investments (i.e., stock selection) with the goal of outperforming a benchmark (such as the S&P 500).

Active managers rely on the following to give them an information edge:

- Analytical research (fundamental and quantitative)
- Market forecasts and trends
- Judgment and experience
- Shifts in the economy
- Changes to the political landscape
- Other factors that may affect specific companies

Passive Investing or Index Investing. Passive or index investing involves investing in a fund that tracks a market index, such as the S&P 500 index.

Price-Earnings Multiples (P/E). The price-earnings or P/E multiple is essentially a metric for how expensive a stock is. It is the ratio of the stock price to earnings per share. The change in P/E represents how much people are willing to pay for corporate fundamentals and the reason it's considered speculative is because it can vary widely over time. When the economy expands, price-earnings multiples tend to increase, and vice versa for a declining market.[15]

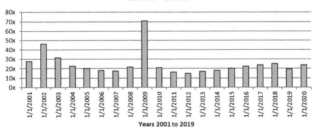

Historical Trailing Price-Earnings Multiple
2001 - 2019

Years 2001 to 2019

☐ Historical Trailing Price Earnings Multiple Average 24.8x

---

15 https://www.multpl.com/. Information is provided "as is" and solely for informational purposes, not for trading purposes or advice, and may be delayed.

Part Three

Invest

Chapter 8

INVESTING IS A MARATHON

DREAM   DESIGN   HIRE   INVEST

Buying stocks is similar in concept to purchasing a home. When you buy a stock, you have no idea if someone else will be willing to pay you more for the stock after you purchased it when you think it's time to sell it. In much the same way, you have no way of knowing whether someone will pay you more for your house when it's time to sell it. At the time of selling the house, one potential buyer might see a house in need of renovation as a great value and opportunity whereas another potential buyer might see the house priced too high and would prefer to pay more for a move-in ready house or can find better value elsewhere. The buyer who sees potential in the house needing renovation looks at other factors, like the location and school district, and analyzes prospects for selling it in the future. They are keeping their focus on the long term and are willing to accept a certain level of risk in exchange for a future profit. On the other hand, the buyer who would prefer to pay more for the move-in ready house is focused on livability and not on a long-term investment.

When we moved to Houston, job growth was higher in Texas than in any other state and unemployment was far below the national average because of the strength of the oil and gas market. This meant we were entering into a hot housing market. Move-in ready houses already had at least five offers on them. Eventually, we found a house for sale in a neighborhood we liked with a good school district; since it was in need of quite a bit of work, we were able to negotiate the price down because there were no other buyers. When the oil and gas market crashed four years later, we were preparing to move to Atlanta and needed to sell the house. Even in the tough housing market, we were able to sell our home for $100,000 profit. Had we purchased a move-in ready house, we likely would have lost a large amount of money; those same houses that had at least five offers on them four years earlier were then being offered at least $300,000 less than their original selling prices.

Throughout this book, we have explored how dreaming, designing, and hiring can help you develop the clarity and confidence you need to invest and ultimately to live the life you want. Now it is time to show you how to invest both on your own and with the guidance of an advisor. There will always be bumps along the road in life, and the same is true for the stock market with better and worse returns, but you are still in the driver's seat. If you execute your financial plan and stay focused on your long-term horizon, you will be living your dream.

Investment in a Perfect World

First, let's start with the perfect world where Goldilocks finds just the right porridge, chair, and bed and there are no market drawdowns or inflation (or bears).

1. Dream. Your dream is to support your lifestyle in retirement and to buy a $2,000,000 second home in 10 years.

2. Design. Your investable assets are all liquid and worth $2,000,000 today. You have no debt and your income perfectly supports your lifestyle expenses. To keep the analysis simple, you are not adding money to your investment portfolio. Here is a quick illustration of your balance sheet

3. Hire. You hire an advisor who understands your dreams. They create models that project out how much money you will need to support your lifestyle when you retire in 10 years and after you purchase your dream house.

4. Invest. Your money is invested in 100% stocks in this perfect Goldilocks world with no volatility, no stock market drawdowns, no inflation, and no cash withdrawals from your portfolio. Your money returns a consistent rate of 7.2% per year for 10 years. Just like magic and thanks to the rule of 72 you will double your $2,000,000 in 10 years to $4,000,000 based on compounded growth rate of your portfolio of 7.2% per year.[16]

In 10 years, not only can you buy your $2,000,000 dream house (there is no inflation, so the price today will be the same in 10 years), you also still have $2,000,000 left to support your lifestyle after you retire, and you live happily ever after!

Investment in the Real World

But, as you know, in the real world there is inflation and—worse than that—there is volatility that didn't exist in our perfect Goldilocks world. Inflation and volatility erode investment performance. The emotions of investors amp up the emotional roller coaster of the stock market just like in "Little Red

16 Rule of 72. Here's how it works. Just divide the number 72 by your annual interest rate. So if your money is earning 7.2% every year, it will double in 10 years. 72 / 7.2% = 10 years. Rule of 72 is an easy back-of-the-envelope way to figure out how long it will take invested money to double given the compounded growth rate (7.2%). This is not a guarantee; nothing about investing is a guarantee. In the real world, return rates aren't usually smooth from year to year or from decade to decade.

Riding Hood." The Big Bad Wolf of volatility is just waiting in the woods, ready to jump out and get you.

Volatility is scary. When markets correct, there is usually a crisis. Short-term investors start to run for the exits at the exact same time, creating complete chaos. The big institutional investors have to sell when something happens because they are measured by short-term performance. These guys are all a bunch of Little Red Riding Hoods, running as fast as they can for the exit. But guess what? If you have a long-term time horizon, you don't have to react when everyone else is reacting. You can hide behind the bush and let the wolf chase after all of those Little Red Riding Hoods while you and your advisor sit back and relax. Your financial plan is like having a magic shield, giving you protection and peace of mind that the other guys don't have.

In reality, yes, market corrections and volatility are crazy, but it's the way the world works; you can't get a higher return without risk. This is the reason why having a financial plan interlinked with your investment portfolio. If you look back over time and keep a level head, you will see how the market always bounces back. With compounding growth, you have a good chance of doubling your money in 10 years as long as you don't react and sell when everyone else is selling. On average historically, the S&P 500's annual returns have been in the area of 10%, which means that stocks have doubled investors' money about every seven years. However, timing is everything, and the market can go up a lot more than 10% over a specific interval; it can also go down a lot more than 10%. Just look at the wild swings we have had over the past year and also the past 50 years since 1969. The gray bar represents the average market return at 10%, but the spread or the standard deviation of that return over the same period has been 16.5% either below or above, which means the historical return of 10% can range within one standard deviation or 68% of the time from the average +/- 16.5% or range from - 6.5% to + 26.5% return. In simpler terms, while on average the S&P 500 historically returns 10% per year, there is a 16% chance returns will fall below -6.5%.

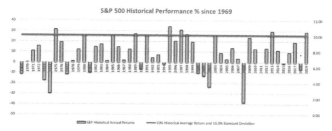

S&P 500 Historical Performance % since 1969

Note: Source Macrotrends Data Download. The annual percentage change of the S&P 500 index back to 1969. Performance is calculated as the % change from the last trading day of each year from the last trading day of the previous year. The current price of the S&P 500 as of July 17, 2020 is 3,224.73

133

We know that volatility is to be expected and is simply part of the investment equation in order to achieve returns above the risk-free rate (the interest an investor would expect to earn from a risk-free investment, treasury bonds as one example). There are no guarantees in the market, but this 10% average has held remarkably steady for a long time. In our real world example, if our portfolio doesn't double in seven years, then we can either wait a while until our portfolio reaches the goal of $4,000,000 so we can afford the $2,000,000 house and fund our lifestyle, or we can purchase a cheaper house.

What investment gets us to this magical compounding return? Simple math and history show us the winning strategy for investing is to invest and own all of the nation's publicly held businesses at a very low cost. The best way to implement this strategy is to buy a fund that holds this all-market portfolio and think about it as the vehicle to achieve your dreams. As we have described above, this fund is called an **index fund**. An index fund is essentially a bucket of stocks designed to mimic the overall performance of the US stock market. It eliminates the risk that comes from picking individual stocks, emphasizing certain market sectors, and manager selection. Only the stock market risk remains. The most popular index is the Standard and Poor's 500 (S&P 500) index fund. One of the easiest and simplest ways to invest in stocks is by buying an index fund for the long term.

"All you had to do was believe in America," Warren Buffett said. "You didn't have to read the **Wall Street Journal.** *You didn't have to look up the price of your stock. You didn't have to pay a lot of money in fees to anybody. You just had to believe that the American miracle was intact."*

There was a testing period after the stock market crash of 1929 where a lot of people "really lost faith," Buffett said. "In the end, the answer is never bet against America." What Wall Street won't tell you is that, while some wealthy people invest in real estate, hedge funds, and other types of investments with high entrance costs, most wealthy people typically invest in simple, low-fee, market-matching index funds. Wall Street can't charge high fees investing in the S&P 500, so it isn't a mystery why they choose not to promote it.

S&P 500 Top 10 Holdings

	Company	Ticker Symbol	Weight %
1	Microsoft Corporation	MSFT	6.0%
2	Apple Inc.	AAPL	6.0%
3	Amazon.com Inc.	AMZN	5.0%
4	Facebook Inc. Class A	FB	2.2%
5	Alphabet Inc. Class A	GOOGL	1.7%
6	Alphabet Inc. Class C	GOOG	1.7%
7	Johnson & Johnson	JNJ	1.5%
8	Berkshire Hathaway Inc. Class B	BRK.B	1.4%
9	Visa Inc. Class A	V	1.2%
10	Procter & Gamble Company	PG	1.2%
11-500	489 other companies in Index		72.2%

As you can see in the chart above, 30% of the S&P 500 index includes some of the best performing companies in the last 10 years. Stock prices tend to run in a certain direction over periods of time, and they have done this repeatedly throughout history.

On average based on historical returns, you might have a high degree of confidence you can double your money in 10 years if you invest 100% in the S&P 500 index as long as you don't pull money out of your portfolio.

For more discussion on S&P 500 revenue growth and earnings per share growth, please see the Appendix.

This is the probabilistic range of outcomes over 10 years of $2,000,000 invested. What these curves show us is the range of outcomes based on 10,000 simulated portfolios with $2,000,000 initially invested based on historical returns and inflation data. You can be 75% confident you might have $2,824,000 blue line in 10 years in real terms and that on average you will have $4,180,000 teal line in 10 years in real terms.[17]

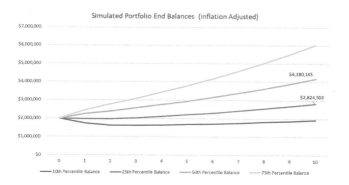

With information from your financial plan (income statement and balance sheet), an advisor constructs a financial forecast based on different time horizons

17 Source: Portfolio visualizer. Assumptions: Monte Carlo simulation results for 10,000 portfolios with $2,000,000 initial portfolio balance using available historical returns data from Jan 1994 to Dec 2019. The historical return for the selected portfolio for this period was 11.35% mean return (9.73% CAGR) with 14.36% standard deviation of annual returns. The simulation results are based on generated nominal returns and specified inflation adjusted withdrawals ($0.00 per year). The simulated inflation model used historical inflation with 2.21% mean and 1.17% standard deviation based on the Consumer Price Index (CPI-U) data from Jan 1994 to Dec 2019. The generated inflation samples were correlated with simulated asset returns based on historical correlations. The available historical data for the simulation inputs was constrained by SPDR S&P 500 ETF Trust (SPY) [Feb 1993–Aug 2020].

and ups and downs (volatility) of the market based on history and asset allocation between stocks and bonds, and discusses with you the gaps, if there are any, in achieving your financial future. An advisor develops multiple goals and prioritizes those goals to give you a "range of outcomes" that will help you define success. This "range of outcomes" gives us the flexibility to allow for volatility!

Manage Risks

As the CFO of your own portfolio, you also have to manage risk. Think back to the biggest financial loss you have ever experienced. What fears or concerns does that bring up for you? Whatever this concern is, it's important to address it. If your dream is to make sure you can sustain your lifestyle into retirement, you need to know the withdrawal rate, which is the estimated percentage of your investment portfolio you're able to withdraw each year from your portfolio throughout retirement without running out of money. Here is the rule of thumb: For a high degree of confidence that you can cover a consistent amount of expenses in retirement (i.e., it should work 90% of the time), aim to withdraw no more than 4% of your investment portfolio in the first year of retirement and then adjust the amount every year for inflation.

Let's look at a hypothetical example. Stephanie and Joseph retire at age 67 with $3,000,000 in lump sum payout from the sale of a business. Stephanie is a conservative investor and Joseph is an aggressive investor, so a balanced portfolio of 50% stocks and 50% intermediate municipal (or "muni") bonds would be best for the couple. Both decide to withdraw 4% of the portfolio per year, or $120,000 per year, for living expenses and would like to leave money to their two grown children. Since Joseph plans on withdrawing an equivalent inflation-adjusted amount from the investment portfolio throughout his retirement, factoring in Stephanie's longer life expectancy of 30 years, this $120,000 serves as his baseline for the years ahead. Each year, the amount of the withdrawal increases by inflation. At the end of 30 years, they have $1 million to leave to their two kids at a 90% confidence level (the gray line) and $2.8 million to leave to their two kids at a 75% confidence level (the teal line).[18] What a difference between a very

---

18 Source: Portfolio visualizer. Monte Carlo simulation results for 10,000 portfolios with $3,000,000 initial portfolio balance using available historical returns data from Jan 2008 to Dec 2019. The historical return for the selected portfolio for this period was 7.41% mean return (6.94% CAGR) with 7.94% standard deviation of annual returns. The simulation results are based on generated nominal returns and specified inflation adjusted withdrawals ($120,000 per year). The simulated inflation model used historical inflation with 1.70% mean and 1.32% standard deviation based on the Consumer Price Index (CPI-U) data from Jan 2008 to Dec 2019. The generated inflation samples were correlated with simulated asset returns based on historical correlations. The available historical data for the simulation inputs was constrained by iShares National Muni Bond ETF (MUB) [Oct 2007–Jul 2020].

good market when the couple starts to withdrawal versus a very bad market when the couple decides to withdrawal. This "range of outcomes" gives us the flexibility to allow for volatility that will give you confidence to allow you to accomplish your dreams.

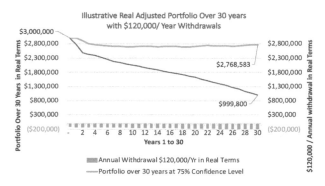

Illustrative Real Adjusted Portfolio Over 30 years with $120,000/ Year Withdrawals

Asset Allocation

In the chapter on hiring, we talked about how advisors can put everything together and model out your financial future based on various asset allocations. Asset allocation is fundamental to the success of a financial plan as it helps you manage volatility. Based on this analysis, we show clients they can withstand fairly significant volatility (risk and reward) and still reach their goals. Asset allocation among the different asset classes such as stocks, bonds, alternatives, and each piece of the pie is usually expressed as a percentage of the whole.

140

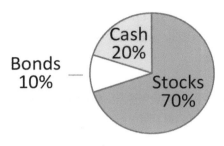

Your asset allocation balances growth and stability. Stocks and bonds offer contrasting advantages and disadvantages. Stocks are growthy investments, but they also are riskier and more volatile. Bonds provide a coupon payment and are typically part of an investment portfolio because they protect part of your portfolio when there is a stock market sell-off. Bonds in a portfolio reduce the volatility but do so at the cost of lower expected returns. Even though bonds provide a nice buffer during market drawdowns, they do not protect you against inflation.

This is where an advisor adds value and partners with you in helping to design your investment plan to the dream. They can help you determine which allocation is best for you depending on your time horizon, financial goals, and how much risk you are comfortable with. For example, if you have high income and live modestly but don't like the volatility of the stock market, you don't have to take as much risk and can be in more conservative investments.

Let's say you are about to retire and want to make sure you don't run out of money but are unsure how much you can spend each year. Based on historical returns and simulated portfolio calculations, if you have $2,000,000 today and are 70 years old, you will spend $100,000 of your portfolio a year adjusted for inflation, which is subtracting from your portfolio. You invest in 40% bonds and 60% stocks at a 75% confidence level you will not run out of money and have $1.2 million to leave to your kids.[19] If the volatility becomes too great and we fall outside that "comfort zone of acceptable outcomes," we can always adjust some of our less-important goals to get back in tolerance.

---

19 Source: Portfolio Visualizer. Assumptions: Monte Carlo simulation results for 10,000 portfolios with $2,000,000 initial portfolio balance using available historical returns data from Jan 2008 to Dec 2019. The historical return for the selected portfolio for this period was 8.06% mean return (7.47% CAGR) with 8.95% standard deviation of annual returns. The simulation results are based on generated nominal returns and specified inflation adjusted withdrawals ($100,000 per year). The simulated inflation model used historical inflation with 1.70% mean and 1.32% standard deviation based on the Consumer Price Index (CPI-U) data from Jan 2008 to Dec 2019. The generated inflation samples were correlated with simulated asset returns based on historical correlations. The available historical data for the simulation inputs was constrained by Vanguard Total Bond Market ETF (BND) [May 2007–Aug 2020].

Illustrative Real Adjusted Portfolio Over 25 years with $100,000/ Year Withdrawals

What makes stocks volatile? It's the price of long-term growth. Oftentimes stocks move up or down because of big-picture factors like interest rate changes, unemployment rate, economic data, earnings expectations, or simply having more buyers than sellers or the opposite more sellers than buyers. We must remember the facts about the long-term trend of markets and the relatively short duration of sell-offs to remind ourselves that, no matter how bad the swings are, we should not let volatility (or our emotions) impact our decision-making. The headlines can cause real anxiety. Look at the biggest and shortest sell-off we've ever experienced in history with COVID-19 in the spring of 2020. We went from experiencing one of the biggest bull markets (meaning it's on the rise and the economy is sound) to one of the biggest bear markets (where the economy is receding and most stocks are declining in value) to back to the biggest bull markets with the Fed flooding the economy with liquidity and work-from-home technology stocks leading the charge. Just like your teenage daughter's mood swings, they are short term and you still love her in the long run.

When it comes to investing in the stock market, you can't be emotional. You have to be prepared to expect the unexpected. We need to make sure you have protection in place so that you can weather the market tantrums. Our brains are working against us when it comes to things like volatility, and we make mistakes. That's why it's so important that your investment plan is synchronized with your personal threshold for risk and your long-term time horizon. If you have faith in and an understanding of how your money is invested (stocks vs. bonds vs. cash), managing volatility will be much easier for you.

There are two important strategies for managing volatility in my experience. The first is to avoid market timing. Market timing is the strategy of making buying or selling decisions of financial assets by attempting to predict future market price movements. The prediction may be based on an outlook of market or economic conditions resulting from technical or fundamental analysis. Unfortunately, some people love to think they can market time and try to sell at the top only to have to get back in at a much higher price. The second is to zig when others zag. Be opportunistic during times of uncertainty, and don't react when everyone else reacts. Don't sell the market just because everyone else is selling the S&P 500. The entire market isn't going to go bankrupt. Individual stocks may go bankrupt, but the US stock market never will. I can say that with 100% confidence.

Core and Satellite Approaches

Now that you have learned the basics about stock market returns and volatility, it's time to put it all together and look at various approaches to investing. To keep things simple, the investment strategy called core and satellite creates an efficient portfolio. Core strategies provide exposure to asset classes that are broadly representative of the market. Examples of core investments include S&P 500 and US fixed income. Satellite strategies have the potential to deliver higher returns derived from skilled active management, which I will help guide you through below. You can invest in a low-cost S&P 500 index fund (NYSE ticker SPY) and then have some play money to invest in aggressive growth stocks.

For someone relatively new to choosing what to invest in, sifting through the many different options can be overwhelming. But don't just do nothing out of frustration. A financial advisor can shepherd you through the maze of investing choices. First, let's review. In developing your financial plan, your advisor should have a good understanding of your dreams, goals, and time horizon and should talk to you about your risk tolerance and risk capacity. An understanding of your risk profile and your financial plan helps advisors determine your investment asset allocation. You should let your advisor know your investment preferences so you can work through different portfolio allocations and the return expectations and risk associated with each choice.

This guide can help you figure out your options and focus your efforts. Richard Thaler, a Nobel prize–winning economist, found that when people have too many options, they tend to avoid making a decision all together. There are any number of asset allocation portfolios one could create to implement an investment plan. I'm here to help you wade through the options and keep it simple by looking at four basic approaches. While they increase in complexity, all are very easy to implement.

As we have already discussed, asset allocation refers to the mix of investments in a portfolio. It describes the proportion of stocks, bonds, and cash that make up any given portfolio. As Jack Bogle, the late founder of Vanguard Group, put it: "The most fundamental decision of investing is the allocation of your assets: How much should you own in stocks? How much should you own in bonds? How much should you own in cash reserve?" Based on a vast amount of historical data, we know how different allocations between stocks and bonds behave over long periods of time.

The decision investors need to make is how much volatility they can stomach while also considering the returns they need to meet their financial goals. Your core may also include a higher percentage of fixed income investments if you are seeking additional capital preservation. You will need to determine how much cash to hold depending on a basic view of the market and your own financial plan. If the market is close to an all-time high, it's better to have cash on sidelines to take advantage of better market conditions. If the market is trading at an all-time low, it's better to invest this cash on the dip to take advantage of corrections.

We can divide core asset allocation models into three broad groups:

Income Portfolio: 70% to 100% in bonds
Balanced Portfolio: 40% to 60% in stocks
Growth Portfolio: 70% to 100% in stocks

For long-term retirement investors, a growth portfolio is generally recommended. If you are seeking greater growth over a long-time horizon, you may want to add more aggressive growth stocks with the fourth option: a satellite portfolio. Satellite investments are based on geography (international stocks), company characteristics (high-growth tech companies), and alternatives (real estate and commodities). If you already have significant risk exposure to your own business, executive compensation plans, or large illiquid holdings, you may want to use core strategies to balance the satellite risk exposures in your overall portfolio.

When you're ready to really *grow* your wealth, you'll need to be more comfortable with higher risk stocks in your satellite portfolio. Let's go a bit deeper into how you can do your own stock research so that you can become a woman who invests with confidence.

Chapter 9

DO YOUR OWN RESEARCH

*"An investment in knowledge
pays the best interest."*
—*Benjamin Franklin*

Investment opportunities are everywhere. Just look around. From the supermarket to the workplace, we encounter and buy products and services all day long. By paying attention to the best ones, we can find companies in which to invest before the professional analysts discover them. If you are a woman reading this book, you have a variant view because men don't know what you buy. Outside of investing in basic materials, which I love because I love international monetary theory and supply and demand (zzz boring, I know), some of my most fun investment ideas have come from looking at the world around me and taking notice of what I buy, do and enjoy. TJ Maxx, Lululemon, Peloton, Zoom, and Wix.com are just a few examples.

Peter Lynch, author of *One Up on Wall Street*, coined some of the best known mantras of modern individual investing strategies. His most famous investment principle is simply, "Invest in what you know." This popularized the economic concept of "local knowledge." Since most people tend to become an expert in certain fields, applying this basic "invest in what you know" principle helps individual investors find good undervalued stocks. Reading this book early in my career taught me how to look at the world around me for investment ideas and helped me land my first job on the buy side working at a hedge fund.

Lynch uses this principle as a starting point for investors. He has also often said that the individual investor is more capable of making money from stocks than a fund manager because they are able to spot good investments in their day-to-day lives before Wall Street. Throughout his two classic investment primers, he has outlined many of the investments he found when he was out with his family, driving around, or making a purchase at the mall. Lynch believes the individual investor is able to do this, too. As women, we have such knowledge about the products, services, and companies that are valuable to the consumer market. With just a few more concepts, you'll be prepared to control your investment by doing your own research.

A few years ago, I started to notice how much LaCroix sparkling water my friends and I were drinking. I really enjoyed the unique flavors in the bright sunny cans, and the grocery shelves were filled with their colorful cases. I naturally looked up to see if the company was public or had shares listed on an exchange so I could buy them. I discovered that the owner of the brand was National Beverage Company and that it was a relatively unknown company. There was no research coverage provided by big Wall Street firms, so I did my normal research and loved the stock. I bought it in the 40s, sold it at 60s, and bought it again in the 50s.

Your own observations about the consumer patterns, branding, and marketing around you will usually be the starting point for your research. Then it's time to do a bit of detective work and to dig deeper into how the company is managed and how others "value" the company. However, just because you enjoy a product or service doesn't necessarily mean it's a good stock to buy. In this section, I want to show you doing your own research on stocks is fun. It can even be a fun family activity. You and your kids will enjoy working together and exploring the world of saving and investing.

Valuing a Company's Stock

When trying to figure out which valuation method to use to value a stock for the first time, most investors will quickly discover the overwhelming number of valuation techniques available to them today. Each stock is different, and each industry sector has unique properties that may require varying valuation approaches. When it comes to investing, my personal style is to look at exactly three areas of a company: fundamental analysis, P/E ratios, and debt and EBITDA metrics.

Fundamental Analysis

When researching an investment, there are typically five documents and an investor presentation. All of these documents are on a company's website under Investors. You'll want to get your hands on them so you can analyze the relative merit of a potential investment. These documents, which you should have no trouble finding, are:

- The Form 10-K. This is the annual filing with the Securities and Exchange Commission (SEC) and is probably the single most important research document available to investors about a company.
- The most recent Form 10-Q. This is the quarterly version of the Form 10-K.
- The Proxy Statement, which includes information on the Board of Directors as well as management compensation and shareholder proposals.
- The most recent annual report. While reading the annual report, you'll want to pay special attention to the letter from the Chairman and CEO and evaluate his or her message yourself. Not all annual reports are created equally.
- Financials going back five or ten years. Several firms prepare this type of information in easy-to-digest formats. Some of the major research houses and products include Morningstar, The Value Line Investment Survey, Standard and Poor's, Moody's, and Yahoo! Finance provides good information as well.

Once we have these documents, we're just getting started to understand the investment opportunity. I'm not here to tell you there is one particular formula to follow but only to show you some of the basics that most sophisticated investors use. It's really up to you to develop your own unique style and investment formula if you plan to pick stocks.

P/E Ratios

There are two primary components of the "value" of the company:

1. The price of the stock
2. The earnings per share of the company

The price of the company's stock can be found on any financial website, like Yahoo! Finance. The earnings of the company will need a bit more research into those above documents you've gathered. You can read the company's quarterly earnings press release and listen to their call, both of which are published publicly, and you can ask yourself these questions:

- Will the company beat earnings expectations in the next quarter or in the next year?
  » If so, what are the catalysts that will cause the company to beat earnings

(e.g., higher revenue, higher margins, lower interest expense, share buybacks, etc.)?

- What's your confidence the company will beat earnings? What's the probability?
- How, when, and why might there be a catalyst that would support higher earnings?
- Where is the company trading relative to its peer group?
  - » If the entire market has seen multiple expansion, then is it fair that this company should too? In other words, is it expensive or cheap relative to itself historically and/or its peers, and can you explain why this might be wrong?
- What's your margin of safety? What can go wrong?
- Can the company repurchase its shares to increase its earnings per share? If the number of shares outstanding decreases, the denominator decreases and earnings per share increases.

Earnings are very important to consider. After all, earnings represent profits, and that's what every business strives for. Earnings are calculated by taking the hard figures into account: revenue, cost of goods sold (COGS), salaries, rent, etc. These are all important to the livelihood of a company. If the company isn't using its resources effectively, it will not have positive earnings, and problems will eventually arise. The value of a company takes both the price of the stock and the earnings of the company into account in a ratio that's known as the "price-earnings ratio" or the "P/E ratio." The price-earnings ratio is also sometimes known as the price multiple or the earnings multiple.

P/E ratio = Price per Share / Earnings per Share

Suppose that a company is currently trading at $43 a share, and its earnings over the last 12 months were $1.95 per share back in 2014. The trailing P/E ratio for the stock could then be calculated as $43/$1.95, or 22.1x.

A low valuation of a stock might be 10 to 12x or less, and a high valuation stock with higher growth prospects might trade at 20 to 35x P/E. The math is pretty straightforward and easy to calculate. And these are exactly the numbers you need to create the story of the stock and know whether it's worth seriously considering as an investment. I had been keeping an eye on the Lululemon stock for a while when I noticed all the women in Houston wore that brand of yoga clothes everywhere around town back in 2014. The company had a choppy first half of the year, including some inventory and management issues.

I pulled all the research documents, calculated the historical P/Es, and bought the LULU stock when it was low in the $40s in 2014. About six months later, the stock was back at $65. Yahoo! Finance reports consensus EPS provided by Thomson Reuters under the Analysts tab equals 22x. LULU is on a January fiscal year-end, which is typical of retailers so that they can capture all of the Christmas shopping season and returns. I felt back in 2014 LULU was going to be a high-growth company and should trade at a higher P/E multiple than 22x.

However, buyer beware, women's apparel is tough business. It's volatile, and there are issues all the time, even with just the assortment not being what women want to buy. You'll notice over time that if the earnings go up and down, it's harder to put a higher P/E on the business because if earnings are more volatile and less consistent they are less predictable. P/Es go up when the story of the stock is getting better, similar to house prices. Why are they going up? Because your house appreciated in value. More people would like to live in your neighborhood with the school district and good jobs in the area.

Calculating valuation is a skill you can practice, and just as with any skill, there's plenty of room to go deeper.

Debt and EBITDA Metrics

The company's balance sheet will reveal how much cash they have and how much debt they have. For instance, in my previous research of Lululemon, I discovered that the company had $870 million in cash with no debt. That cash is not included in the equity or market value or price of the stock, so we have to subtract the cash to get to the enterprise value. If the company had debt we would add the debt to the market value to calculate the enterprise value. Enterprise value is the total value of the entire company, including market value of a business plus the sum of all debt less cash. Back in 2014, LULU had about $7.7 billion market value less $870 million in cash, which brought the enterprise value to $6.8 billion. Plus, the company was generating

$440 million in free cash flow a year and growing. Cash flow, or EBITDA, is earnings before interest, taxes, depreciate, and amortization. Evaluating the entire total value of the company to its cash flow may better represent a company's firm value.

Doing that initial research and knowing the price and earnings is only part of the picture. You also want to know if they have cash to help them survive a downturn, or if they're severely leveraged, which means if the company has too much debt and there is serious downturn too much debt might make it more difficult for the company to weather the storm of a recession and would easily cross into bankruptcy before you invest any money with them!

Diversifying Your Investments

Common wisdom tells us that we should diversify our investment portfolios because it's foolish to put all our money in one stock. If you've found a company you like, you can next look at competition. Let's stick with our Lululemon example. If you already own some Lululemon gear, you probably own some other athletic gear and know who the competition is. I own some Patagonia, New Balance, Adidas, and Under Armour running clothes, plus some cheap stuff I bought on a running shoes website. Patagonia and New Balance are private, so it's not listed on the stock market. Adidas is German, so it's also not listed on the US stock market. Adidas, and Under Armour are public companies that are in the athletic gear space. They may not specialize in women's athleisure as much as Lululemon does, but it's worth looking into competitors on Yahoo! Finance.

And it's just as important to consider the consequences of a lack of diversification if we all work for one company or one industry. Women are natural at diversifying because we're involved in so many aspects of life: our own employment, our kids' education and activities, our friends' hobbies and lifestyles, and our husbands' work and pursuits. We see the full spectrum of industries, and if we look at the patterns we may be surprised at the opportunities we find.

In 2015, my husband and I were catching up with our friend who runs a major endowment for a high-ranking private university. He told us the biggest issue the school is facing is that the school's capacity is relatively fixed in the short term. It can't build new buildings or hire more teachers to expand the class size to match the growth of talented students who would otherwise attend that school. This is the reason why so many of us parents are stressed out about our kids getting into a good college and the skyrocketing tuition prices (around 5 to 6% per year currently). College is increasingly becoming more and more expensive and difficult to get into.

By chance, I came across a company that is trying to use technology to address this capacity issue. It's called 2U (NASDAQ ticker TWOU) and provides universities the ability to expand their graduate classes by allowing students to take classes from home or from other parts of the country. For example, if you live in Houston and your passion is to go to USC Marshall Business School in Los Angeles, you can take classes remotely and just visit the campus once a quarter for socializing and networking. The company provides high-quality video and technology to allow for interaction via the internet; it's the backbone to the setup. They get half of the student's tuition, and the university gets the other half. Pretty brilliant. You can bet I followed that paper trail and calculated the valuation of that company!

Why NOW Is the Time to Manage Your Own Money

Because our world is changing so quickly, there are constantly new investment opportunities to consider. An analyst once came to our office to discuss the company Mobileye, which created sensors and software in the computer in your car that allows you to back up without hitting a child or park without hitting the car next to you. When this technology came out, I wanted to sell both of our cars to get it because my biggest fear as a parent is accidentally hitting a child when backing up. But the stock was expensive because the company also had a long runway of growth with autonomous driving. I worked on understanding the company, personally invested in it, and made a lot of money. It traded at 50x revenue but only 85x P/E because margins where 80% due to it being a software company. I also presented the company to our investment committee. After a few times pushing the stock, my boss came into my office with my colleague and told me in so many words that I was crazy to like Mobileye because of its high valuation. A few months later, my boss asked me to present the idea in front of a hundred of our clients as a "see what's next" stock, which Mobileye represents.

Apparently, he had completely forgotten about calling me stupid, in so many words.

This is just one type of technology change that a woman could see coming a mile away. And here are some of the other long-term areas of change that I'm keeping my eye on:

Clean air and carbon reduction
Water scarcity
Sustainability
Waste management and recycling
Emerging market infrastructure
Energy efficiency
Automation and robotics
Emerging market health care
Obesity
Education services
Retirement planning
Safety and security

If you have any personal connection with companies in these types of industries where change is happening now, you have the perfect opportunity to dig into those three areas of a company we've just covered in this chapter: fundamental analysis, P/E ratios, and debt and EBITDA metrics.

Becoming a Woman In Charge of Her Future

Investing wisely not only helps you make money but is also fun because it allows you to tell other people how you became interested in a company and how the company improved your life in some way, making you want to be part owner of the story that can help improve the lives of others. When I decided to quit drinking Diet Coke for health reasons and discovered how much I loved LaCroix sparkling flavored water, I didn't know why I loved the drink so much until I read the shareholder letter written by the founder. He invested in a bright, beautifully designed can to remind customers of being on vacation every time they drank from it. That's the power of a great brand!

Investing teaches you a lot about business: brand marketing, management systems, and financial management. Does management make a bunch of excuses for bad performance like a kid who is trying to get out of getting into trouble? Or are they really hard on themselves and say we can do better even after having a great quarter? Does management admit that technology or higher competition is hurting their business, but they have an actionable plan that makes sense to you for them to recover from this threat?

166

Investing is really powerful and clear. You're either right or wrong, and you get paid only if you're right in terms of making a good investment decision. If you're wrong and you lose money, you must learn from those mistakes so that you decrease your chances of making the same mistake twice. Investing teaches you a lot about life and business. And, really, we can actually apply investing philosophy to our personal lives, too. With a financial model, you are working towards exceeding, beating, and avoiding missing expectations. And you can have your own "life model," where you have a plan in place or focus on what is important so that you can work towards a goal and not waste time on meaningless tasks like gossip and comparing ourselves to others.

What does it mean to you to find something that's "cheap" to buy? Finding a bargain is fun, but does it create meaningful long-term value in your life? A savvy financial investor doesn't recommend that you buy a stock simply because it's cheap. The company is cheap for a reason. Sometimes sweaters are on sale because no one likes the style or color. You might buy it because it's cheap, but if you never wear it and it sits in your closet, you are out the $50. If you buy a stock because it is cheap, and the company isn't able to create value, the stock will stay cheap. We call this type of investment a "value trap."

Good companies have good brands, and we want to create our own good personal brands. Everything we learn in researching and valuing a stock can provide insight into our own lives. If you don't develop a good personal brand, you may be perceived as not knowing what you personally would like to achieve in life. In fact, even in writing this book, I decided that I had to go through a brand exercise if I wanted to build a successful company. My mission in life is to help women become better investors and achieve their best life.

Learning how to invest has given me a rich life, a better life than I would ever have achieved if I had kept my head down, gotten good grades, and just worked really hard at my job. I learned from investing that I can aim high, be more aggressive with my best ideas, rebound from setbacks, develop my weaknesses, leverage my uniqueness, and exploit my creativity. The stock market is one of the best wealth generators out there, and it has made me more successful in my career than I would have ever imagined. I want to share this gift with you.

The Power of a Woman's Conviction

I'll admit that it's hard to take the time to meaningfully engage with families and spend enough time researching stocks. Yet, I feel called to reach out to generations of women, my own generation and the generations of young women we're raising. Maybe women out there will become interested in looking at the world through the lens of investing. Maybe it will even encourage their daughters to work on Wall Street and monetize their unique views. From a management perspective, trying to engage more women to invest and manage their money is a blue ocean. Neither technology nor higher competition can hurt my business as an advisor, and as an investor I keep looking for new and amazing companies like Peloton, Zoom, and Wix.com. Women prefer working with an advisor they trust, and that's often another successful woman. The investment world needs more women. Among 7,410 portfolio managers of US open-end mutual funds, just over 9% were women as of March 31, 2015, according to a study by investment researcher Morningstar, Inc. Women manage less than 3% of mutual funds exclusively.[20]

---

20 Daisy Maxey, July 6, 2015, "Where Are the Female Fund Managers?" *The Wall Street Journal.*

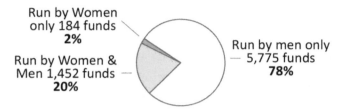

You've Got Males
Gender breakdown of 7,410 Portfolio Managers
of US Mutual Funds

Run by Women
only 184 funds
2%

Run by Women &
Men 1,452 funds
20%

Run by men only
— 5,775 funds
78%

Note: As of March 31, 2015 US Mutual funds only.
Source. Morningstar.

I was part of the Wall Street club. I had a portable track record, but when I left my job as a portfolio manager with a ranking of 16% return and second-highest performance out of the set of portfolio managers at the fund, I couldn't find another job. I had interviews at funds that I thought were sure bets where I didn't get an offer. I can't say for sure that it was because I'm a woman, but that was the impression I had from the process.

I believe that, if we can increase women's engagement in investing, we can encourage more women to start businesses and advance our social status. Investing allows us to drive a redistribution of power, capital, and opportunity. Learning how to find an idea and do research on a stock shouldn't just be left to the big boys on Wall Street. You are only enriching them with your money. Our money and the markets are complex, and in fact, Wall Street firms make it overly complex so that they can charge you unnecessarily high fees and make themselves rich. Maybe you would just rather have someone do it for you, which is completely understandable, but I want you educated enough to know how to ask good questions and avoid being overcharged.

Learning how to invest will help you understand what venture capitalists, or early-stage investors, look for to invest in your own startup, which will help you raise money or gain career support when you want to start your own business or take your business to the next level. Most importantly, learning about the business, economic, and debt cycles and how these impact investing will help you feel more confident in your investment, your future, and your family.

Conclusion

I hope that, by reading this book, you see through the complexity of investing and realize how simple it really is. Wall Street takes great pride in using dense language and making investing complex because it makes them appear smart. Their big talk is meant to intimidate you. Simplicity is really all about having the sophistication and desire to invite everyone in. You deserve a seat at the table and the opportunity to pursue your dreams.

Now it's time for the hard part: execution. The first and easiest action item is to find a good photo of your dream and look at it every day. Put it in a place where you will see it first thing in the morning. Going forward, your responsibility is to carve out time each day to focus on your financial plan, no matter how chaotic or crazy your day-today schedule gets. Figuring out what is important to you and how to fund it will give you the clarity and confidence needed to make decisions about your financial future. The secret to success is that you have to want it. You need to be proud of your dreams and pour yourself into them every day, completely. Sell your dreams to your husband, kids, and friends. Talk about what you want. Share your story. Don't let anyone else shape your future. If you have determination, you will become what you were meant to be.

I'm writing this book so my kids can see their mother taking a risk. I know there will be criticism and judgment, but I'm proud of my track record and am excited to have the courage and confidence to take something I really believe to the next level. I'm proud of my dream, which is to engage women in investing in their wealth. I hope you will take what you have learned here and follow your own dreams. It's time to invest in yourself and your financial future.

Appendix

Oftentimes, when it comes to investing, investors lose sight of the eternal principle that shareholder gains must match the business gains of the company. The late Jack Bogle, who started Vanguard Group, breaks down expected annual returns of the US stock market into the following components.

Market Returns = Dividend Yield + Earnings Growth +/- Changes in the P/E Ratio.

Dividends and earnings are the fundamental portion of stock market returns while the change in the price-to-earnings (P/E) ratio is the speculative portion of returns. The change in P/E represents how much people are willing to pay for corporate fundamentals and the reason it's considered speculative is because it can vary widely over time.

As mentioned previously, the average annual returns of the S&P 500 historically has been 10%, but with years of outperformance and years with underperformance. The excess return can be contributed to speculative returns depending on investors' willingness to either pay higher prices or sell at lower prices for each dollar of earnings.

Here's a look at how Bogle's data looks historically:

Dividend yield has averaged 1.9% from 2001 to 2019, as shown by the graph. S&P 500 dividend yield—(12 month dividend per share) / price.[21]

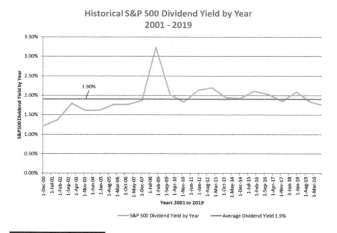

21 Source: https://www.multpl.com/s-p-500-dividend-yield. Yields following June 2020 (including the current yield) are estimated based on 12-month dividends through June 2020, as reported by S&P. Information is provided "as is" and solely for informational purposes, not for trading purposes or advice, and may be delayed.

Earnings growth has averaged 16% per year from 2001 to 2019, as shown by the graph.[22]

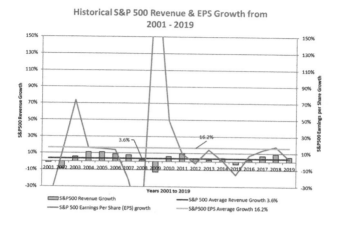

Historical S&P 500 Revenue & EPS Growth from 2001 - 2019

22 Source. https://www.multpl.com/s-p-500-sales-growth. https://www. multpl.com/s-p-500-earnings. Information is provided "as is" and solely for informational purposes, not for trading purposes or advice, and may be delayed.

Historical Trailing P/E multiple and growth, as show by the graph.[23]

23 Source: https://www.multpl.com/s-p-500-pe-ratio. Information is provided "as is" and solely for informational purposes, not for trading purposes or advice, and may be delayed.

CPSIA information can be obtained
at www.ICGtesting.com
Printed in the USA
LVHW020110151120
671611LV00011B/536